SEMINAR STUDIES IN HISTORY

W9-ADW-829

The Origins of the Second World War

R. J. Overy

LONGMAN
London and New York

ADDISON WESLEY LONGMAN LIMITED
Edinburgh Gate, Harlow, Essex CM20 2JE, England
and Associated Companies throughout the world.

Published in the United State of America
by Addison Wesley Longman Inc., New York

First published 1987
Twelfth impression 1996

Set in 10/11pt Baskerville (Linotron)
Produced through Longman Malaysia, PP

ISBN 0-582-35378-5

British Library Cataloguing in Publication Data

Overy, R. J.
    The origins of the Second World War.
    — (Seminar studies in history)
    1. World War, 1939–1945 — Causes
    I. Title   II. Series
    940.53'11   D741

    ISBN 0-582-35378-5

Library of Congress Cataloging in Publication Data

Overy, R. J.
    The origins of the Second World War.
    (Seminar studies in history)
    Bibliography: p.
    Includes index.
    1. World War, 1939–1945 — Causes. 2. Europe —
Politics and government — 1918–1945. I. Title.
II. Series.
D741.084   1986   940.53'11   86–3028
ISBN 0–582-35378-5

Contents

Contents

Part Three: Assessment

Seminar Studies in History
Founding Editor: Patrick Richardson

Introduction

The Seminar Studies series was conceived by Patrick Richardson, whose experience of teaching history persuaded him of the need for something more substantial than a textbook chapter but less formidable than the specialised full-length academic work. He was also convinced that such studies, although limited in length, should provide an up-to-date authoritative introduction to the topic under discussion as well as a selection of relevant documents and a comprehensive bibliography.

Patrick Richardson died in 1979, but by that time the Seminar Studies series was firmly established, and it continues to fulfil the role he intended for it. This book, like others in the series, is therefore a living tribute to a gifted and original teacher.

Note on the System of References:
A bold number in round brackets (**5**) in the text refers the reader to the corresponding entry in the Bibliography section at the end of the book. A bold number in square brackets, preceded by 'doc'. [**doc. 6**] refers the reader to the corresponding item in the section of Documents, which follows the main text.

ROGER LOCKYER
General Editor

Acknowledgements

We are grateful to Macmillan Accounts and Administration Ltd for permission to reproduce extracts from pp 332–3, 416–7 *The Life of Neville Chamberlain* by Keith Feiling.

We are grateful for permission to reproduce table and maps from the following: Map on page 61 based on map from *Atlas of the 20th Century History* by Richard Natkiel, Bison Books, 1985; table on page 49 adapted from page 21 of *The Air War 1939–1945* by R. J. Overy, Europa, 1980; map on page 12 based on map from *Empires in the Balance* by H. P. Willmott, copyright © 1982, H. P. Willmott, Naval Institute Press.

Preface

It might, with some justice, be asked 'Why another book on the Second World War?' I have two excuses. First of all the whole subject has in the last ten years undergone something of a transformation. German ambitions have been reassessed; the nature of appeasement more kindly evaluated; and the importance of economic rivalry and domestic unrest brought firmly into the open. This now makes it possible to assess the outbreak of war in Europe in 1939, and its development by 1941 into world war, within a broader explanatory framework; and also to see why statesmen at the time took the decisions they did, not knowing, as we do, what the consequences of these decisions might be. Secondly, I have tried to provide an interpretation rather than a strict narrative of events. This conforms with the overall purpose of the series, which is to present an analytical rather than a chronological treatment; and it allows the book to address the central question of why war broke out when it did. It is all too tempting to simplify the outbreak of war as the result of one critical event after another producing an inevitable slide to war. There is an element of factual determinism here which exaggerates the importance of Germany and minimises the role of other powers or the system in which they all operated. I have tried in the following pages to open up new perspectives on the outbreak of war and to avoid distorting the realities of the international system.

It may nevertheless seem an impertinence to offer such a brief interpretation, and I am all too aware of its deficiencies. I should like to express a general acknowledgement of my debt to other historians whose work I have compressed and simplified here, but which cannot be given either the space or the recognition it deserves. My thanks also go to those colleagues who have discussed, and often disagreed with, the ideas presented here; and to Roger Lockyer for his kind advice and editorial guidance.

Richard Overy
July 1985

vii

Part One: The Background

1 Explaining the Second World War

The Second World War was once a simple event to explain. If it did not exactly boil down to one word – Hitler – the war was nevertheless the Germans' war. Unlike the war of 1914, that of 1939 had a simple reducible core. Germany provoked war deliberately to overturn the Versailles Settlement of 1919 and win the continental hegemony denied her in 1914. Moreover the Germany of 1939 was led by a party committed to a demonstrably evil cause. Fighting Germany, and later Italy and Japan, was to fight on the side of good in the defence of democracy and freedom, against what President Roosevelt called 'the forces endeavouring to enslave the entire world'.

For all its simplicity there is much to recommend this view. Without Hitler's restless quest for empire, war might have been avoided. If the western powers had not been faced with an accumulation of crisis after crisis in central Europe, which built up almost irresistible pressure for conflict by 1939, German aims might have been accommodated in the international system without war. This is, of course, a very large 'if'. In practice the outbreak of war was a great deal more complicated than this. Historians cannot even agree on the nature of the pressures that pushed Hitler towards war. While some see a clear intention on his part to launch wars of aggression, based on the ideas of racial struggle and world empire expressed in Hitler's writing and speeches, others emphasise the importance of functional explanations: that the Nazi leaders were forced into war in 1939 through fear of domestic unrest and economic crisis brought about by the excessive cost of rearmament. Nor can agreement be reached on the kind of war Hitler launched: total war which required the full use of the nation's resources to fight the great powers for world status; or *Blitzkrieg*, short opportunistic wars, designed to avert domestic political pressure by using a minimum of military resources for each short campaign.

Arguments such as these mask a more important problem in explaining the outbreak of war. By concentrating on Germany we are in danger of forgetting that wars do not take place in a vacuum. Germany was part, and quite a small part, of an international system. German statesmen reacted to problems and stimuli over which, in many cases, they had no control. Hitler planned to subvert a structure of world power for which Germany had very little responsibility except that she had lost, rather than won, the First World War. To understand the outbreak of war in Europe in 1939, and its extension within two years to world war, it is necessary to look at the international structure as a whole, its weaknesses and strengths, and the character and motives of the major powers that comprised it.

It must not be forgotten that war in 1939 was declared by Britain and France on Germany, and not the other way round. A large part of any explanation for the war must rest on this central point. Why did the two western powers go to war with Germany? Immediately the question is put this way round, the role of Germany assumes a new and very different perspective. France and Britain had complex interests and motives for war. They, too, had to take decisions on international questions with one eye on public opinion and domestic politics and another on potential enemies elsewhere. The traditional picture of the western democracies acting as honest brokers in world affairs, vainly trying to uphold the spirit of the Covenant of the League of Nations and the strategy of 'collective security' in the face of totalitarian pressure can no longer be upheld. Nor can the view that saw Chamberlain and his cabinet as 'Guilty Men', honest but incompetent appeasers, willing to give the dictators what they wanted until forced by the moral indignation of popular opinion to fight. Instead historians now emphasise that French and British foreign policy in the 1930s was the product of a complex interplay of domestic and international pressures and interests which cannot be adequately subsumed in the popular notion of appeasement. It was in fact, as A. J. P. Taylor pointed out to public dismay in 1961, old-fashioned balance-of-power politics.

The significance of Taylor's argument was that it forced people to see that British and French policy before 1939 was governed primarily by *raisons d'état*, and only secondarily by moral considerations. In other words the British and the French, just like the Germans, were anxious to preserve or extend their power, and safeguard their economic interests, by a variety of means, some much less scrupulous than others. If, in the end, this meant going to war to preserve Franco-British power and prestige, it also meant finding ways of containing or accommodating other powers in a system still dominated by British and French interests. If Chamberlain has not been completely exonerated by recent historiography, appeasement now seems a far less reprehensible strategy than it did a generation ago. Indeed it can now be seen to be very much in the mainstream of the British diplomatic tradition.

When the explanation for the outbreak of war moves beyond Germany to Britain and France, it at once assumes a global significance. Both the western powers were possessors of empires that stretched across the world. They faced problems not just in central Europe but in the Near East, the Middle East and throughout Africa. The interests of these areas had to be balanced against those nearer home. In the Far East the imperial powers came directly into contact with the two major Pacific powers, Japan and the United States, who both had divergent interests of their own. In Asia and the Middle East Britain and France looked warily towards Soviet Russia and the unpredictable effects of international Communism. In areas remote from Europe the German threat was peripheral, to say the least. British diplomacy was based on a global strategy of which the German question formed a part, and until 1935 a subordinate part. If France was more immediately concerned with German revisionism, she was also a major imperial power threatened by the rise of Mussolini's Italy in the Mediterranean, and by the insecurity of her African and Asian empire. It was the global character of these responsibilities which eventually turned a conflict in Europe over German power into a world war.

Holding all the powers loosely together was the international economy. With the growth of world trade and investment, economic questions impinged on diplomacy in a very direct way. The distribution of the economic spoils, the rise and fall of the international business cycle, deeply affected political decisions and involved all the powers, willy-nilly, in a constant round of economic argument. The powers were compelled to bind their diplomatic and economic interests more closely together. Much of the recent history on the outbreak of war has exposed the importance of 'economic diplomacy', or 'economic appeasement'. There is no doubt that economic rivalry and economic dependence played a major part in the international crisis of the 1930s, adding a new dimension to conflicts which have hitherto been regarded more as the product of military and territorial ambition, or the defence of status and prestige.

There are strong echoes here of the war of 1914. That is not to say that the war of 1914–18 or the post-war settlement at Versailles in any direct sense *caused* the outbreak of the Second World War. But both conflicts were the product of an age of rapid political and diplomatic change which provided the context within which specific crises had to be confronted. Both wars to be fully understood have to be set against this background.

In the years before 1914 the international system was faced with growing crisis. For most of the nineteenth century the major European powers, guided first by Metternich, then by Bismarck, had worked together in a loose concert, designed to maintain the existing distribution of power among the traditional great powers, and to prevent a return to the warfare and political uncertainty of the revolutionary years. Though there were plenty of minor disagreements, there was a broad consensus among the ruling class groups who dominated foreign policy about the need to maintain a balance of power. With the rise of Germany and the United States, the modernisation of Tsarist Russia and Europe's rapid industrialisation, the equilibrium was undermined. In the search for greater security and economic advantage the European powers looked to imperialism. Some like Britain and France, had old-established empires and could build upon them, hesitantly and rather incoherently, in order to enhance their power. Other states rapidly followed, deeming empire to be the explanation for British economic strength and international preponderance. By the 1890s the concert had been replaced by intense diplomatic and economic rivalry, and the growth of a system of fixed alliances. Though the powers still could, and did, co-operate to solve international crises, they resorted increasingly to secret diplomacy, exclusive treaties and, in the end, to rearmament (**79**).

None of this made the outbreak of war inevitable, but it made it much more likely. So, too, did the sharp changes in domestic politics. By the 1890s the tide of democracy and nationalism could no longer be ignored. The traditional ruling houses of Europe found themselves faced with the prospect of the imminent collapse of the old political structure through pressure from middle-class democrats and nationalists and the new working class thrown up by economic growth. International crisis thus assumed a new dimension. War, or the prospect of war, might destroy the old regimes altogether, or might, it was argued, give them a renewed lease of life. Faced with such a choice the Habsburgs, under mounting pressure from nationalists within the Empire and without, opted for war in July 1914 rather than accept the final erosion of Habsburg power. For once, feeble efforts at concerted action by the other powers broke down. The Serbian crisis interlocked with the wider system of rivalries and alliances, and could then not be reversed. By August 1914 all the great powers were at war for the first time since 1815.

At the end of the war Allied statesmen hoped to be able to turn the clock back to the nineteenth-century equilibrium, to a world of 'progress and harmony' (**143**). The defeat of the most threatening new power, Germany, contributed to this sense that the old concert could be resurrected, operated now by the two powers committed to peace, Britain and France. The peace settlement at Versailles was drawn up on these lines. The League of Nations, established in 1919, was the formal part of the system, dependent, like Metternich's Congress System, on the goodwill and self-restraint of the major powers. It was symbolised by the Locarno Treaty of 1925 in which the enemies of 1918 now agreed mutually to guarantee their frontiers against aggression; and by the Kellogg-Briand pact signed in Paris four years later condemning the use of force to resolve conflict. There was also widespread popular support for peace. Pacifist movements drew strength from the new spirit of reconciliation and internationalism; everywhere there was widespread revulsion against the prospect of another major war.

Yet the statesmen who dominated the international system in the 1920s shared a common set of assumptions which could be traced directly back to the world of imperialism and economic rivalry in which they had been brought up before 1900. The year 1918 had been a dividing line of sorts, but not a decisive one. In many cases diplomacy was still dominated by the small specialised élites which ran the foreign offices and diplomatic corps before the war. They all shared the view that the international system was dominated by a small group of great powers, and that the desirable course was to establish, by agreement if possible, some sort of balance between them. Though many politicians shared the revulsion against war, a willingness to resort to force *in extremis* was an essential part of the balance and conformed with the still powerful role of the military in European public life. Most statesmen subscribed, to a greater or lesser degree, to a sense of racial and cultural superiority. In the inter-war years there was nothing exclusively German about this. It was widely assumed that European culture was more enlightened and progressive than that of other races. Outside Europe white rule was held to be in the interest of everybody, ruler and subject alike. Imperialism had its practical side as well. It

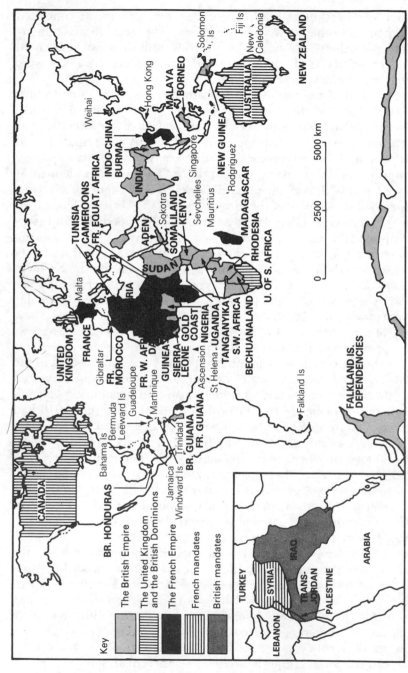

The British and French empires between the two world wars

Key

The British Empire

The United Kingdom
and the British Dominions

The French Empire

French mandates

British mandates

provided an outlet for emigration and trade from Europe, and gave guaranteed access to markets and raw materials. Although many of the assumptions about empire were illusory, this crude geo-political view was deeply rooted in the European mind. The physical possession of territory was still considered a vital interest, a source of prestige and a key to economic growth. In 1937 Neville Chamberlain, the British Prime Minister, argued that in a united empire 'lies the seat of our influence in the world' (**142**).

Just as the values of the pre-war world survived into the 1920s, so too did its problems. In practice the equilibrium of the post-war period masked the continuing fragility of the international system. The war had brought about dramatic changes but had solved little. The old dynastic states of central and eastern Europe had disap-peared, but the problems of nationalist rivalry there and the ques-tion of German and Russian power had been postponed rather than resolved. Although Britain and France were the direct beneficiaries of the war, the problems of being the major imperial powers had multiplied. Both empires reached their fullest extent in the 1920s with the acquisition of German colonies and the break-up of what had been left of the Turkish Empire. But both empires were now under attack by those same forces, nationalism and political liberalism, which had undermined the stability of pre-1914 Europe. In the Middle East, which both Britain and France viewed as vital to the preservation of their global influence, long-standing conflicts in Palestine, Egypt and Syria were now joined with new demands for political independence. Both the European powers were committed to empires whose security and integrity it was difficult to defend. Only the weakness of the defeated powers, and Russia's temporary eclipse, disguised this fact.

For much of the 1920s international affairs were conducted in a vacuum. Britain and France achieved a predominance quite out of proportion to their real strengths because of the temporary unwillingness or inability of the other powers to intervene decis-ively in world politics. The great-power system was played with only two of the major states committed fully to maintaining it. The position of the Soviet Union illustrates this. In the after-math of the Bolshevik Revolution, Russia was plunged into internal political crisis. Although Lenin and Trotsky hoped that 1917 would be a signal to workers throughout Europe to rise and overthrow their governments, the post-war revolutionary threat subsided, leaving Russia exposed and isolated. Her reduced weight in the international scales was confirmed by her defeat at Polish hands in 1920. By 1924 Stalin had modified the effort to export Communism and spoke instead of 'socialism in one country'. The Soviet Union deliberately cut itself off from the rest of the international system. Stalin's priority was to prevent war again on Russian soil and to avoid any diplomatic entanglements likely to bring such a risk about. There is no doubt that Russia possessed great potential strength, and that the other powers underestimated the Communists' ability to create a powerful military and economic state. But in the 1920s Russia no longer played the part in great-power calculations that she had done before 1914.

The same was true, though for very different reasons, of the United States. America had begun before 1914 to exert increasing influence, particularly in the Pacific area, in international affairs. When, in 1917, President Wilson brought the United States into the war, and dominated the post-war peace settlement, it seemed that European power was destined to give way to American. Yet a year after the end of the war the United States turned its back on Europe. Congress refused to ratify the Versailles Treaty or to join the League of Nations. The mood of American public opinion was strongly isolationist. The feeling was widespread that the United States had been led into war by profiteers and bankers in order to shore up the French and British empires, whose role in world affairs Americans deeply distrusted. Although there was no shortage of goodwill on the part of the United States, demonstrated in the efforts to resolve German financial difficulties in the 1923 inflation crisis and again in 1931, the major priority of American foreign policy was to avoid fighting another war for Europe. Yet the United States had become by the 1920s the world's largest economy, backed up by vast material resources and a large population. Like the Soviet Union she possessed great potential military and economic strength, but chose, for domestic reasons, not to exert it in the international arena (**95**).

The source of American strength was economic power. Inexorably, with the onset of industrialisation, there was a growing correlation between economic and diplomatic power. War itself was now industrialised. France and Britain were, in relative terms, declining economies. Britain's share of world trade in manufactured goods was 46 per cent in 1870, but was only 25 per cent by 1914. France's economic growth before 1914 was slower than Britain's, and only half that of Germany's. As new economies developed and grew, so the whole pattern of the international system was thrown into flux. Until economic potential was fully

8

realised it was impossible to stabilise the system. America was a rising economic power which sooner or later would exercise her strength internationally. But so too were Japan and Germany and Italy. All three were new industrial economies, with high rates of growth. Although German economic strength was temporarily broken in 1918, it rapidly revived so that by 1928 Germany was almost as economically powerful as she had been in 1914. By the 1920s, partly because of Britain's involvement in the war, Japan had become the major economy in east and south Asia. In Italy Mussolini's early years of rule coincided with a great upsurge in Italian trade and output. Sooner or later these states, too, like the United States and Russia, would have to be incorporated into the old great-power system.

The very speed of these changes contributed to undermining the ability of the powers, any powers, to secure peace and social progress on their own terms. Within thirty or forty years the social structure and political systems of Europe and its imitators were transformed. Slow evolution was superseded by rapid change; the narrow political nation was replaced by mass politics which, in some cases, placed an intolerable strain on the existing political system. In Germany and Italy it threw up new radical authoritarian movements hostile to the old system yet deeply distrustful of the 'liberal capitalism' borrowed from the west. In Japan it touched off a militarist nationalism which sought to harness Japan's new economic strength to new political ambitions abroad. All these groups were infected with the ideology of imperialism and cultural superiority, whose manifestation in the form of British and French power they were committed to contest.

In the era of the two world wars, against a background of social and political transformation, international relations were in transition. Stability might have been achieved by concerted action based around a shared interest in securing peace as it had been in the nineteenth century. Or it might have been achieved through the existence of powers so strong that they could impose their will on the whole system, as has been the case since 1945. But neither of these things happened. Instead there was a growing contradiction between the existing international system and the reality of power, made more dangerous by the restless political forces released by economic modernisation and the rise of mass politics. This fact did not directly cause the war of 1939 or 1941, but it created an unstable context for the conduct of foreign affairs, and generated ambitions that made war more probable.

9

Part Two: Analysis

2 The International Crisis

During the 1920s diplomacy was conducted against a background of relative stability. The victor powers, France and Britain, played a dominant role, the one in Europe the other outside it. The 1920s were the heyday of liberal, imperial politics, based around the League of Nations and the notion of 'collective security' which it was supposed to represent [**doc. 1**]. This was a system in which, in theory, all the powers would co-operate together to prevent war by bringing joint pressure to bear on any potential aggressor. But because of the isolation or weakness of so many of the major powers during the 1920s the ability of the system to provide effective security was never severely tested.

To underline the commitment to peace and the rational, restrained pursuit of self-interest that it required, the powers sought firm guarantees that would embody the spirit of the League Covenant. In the 1922 Washington Treaty Britain, Japan and the United States agreed to limit naval armaments. The League itself sought positive ways to honour the undertaking to disarm expressed in Article 8 of the Covenant, culminating in the Disarmament Conference which met at Geneva in 1932. In 1925 Germany was invited into the League and at Locarno an agreement was made between the powers that the frontier settlement in the west secured in 1919 should be binding on all. A further commitment was made in the (unratified) Four-Power Pact signed in Rome in June 1933, where the European powers again reiterated the spirit of Locarno and the League by an undertaking to restrain from dangerous unilateral initiatives in Europe and to co-operate together. The direct beneficiaries of all this were the British and the French, who were able to keep their world-wide interests intact, while maintaining the fiction of collective action to preserve peace and international stability.

The collapse of the League

The first cracks in the 'liberal' diplomatic system were brought about by the collapse of the world economy in 1929. The great depression that followed encouraged the growth of protectionist, isolationist policies that exposed the weakness of collective action. As the major powers scrambled to protect their own economic interests, often at the expense of smaller and poorer economies, the spirit of co-operation and mutual aid evaporated. As the depression deepened the western powers cut back more sharply on military spending, which only served to weaken further the international system. In Germany and Japan, countries hit particularly severely by the slump, domestic politics became dominated by radical nationalist groups who demanded an active foreign policy to help overcome their economic difficulties, and to exploit the temporary inaction of the west as it tried to cope with the economic crisis.

The first challenge to the League was made by Japan when, in September 1931, its army invaded the Chinese province of Manchuria and set up there a puppet state, Manchukuo, under Japanese control. Japanese pressure on the Chinese state had grown throughout the 1920s. China was in political chaos following the end of Manchu rule in 1911. The government was faced with a revolutionary threat from Chinese Communism, but was also weakened by provincial disunity and conflict between rival warlords. Given this weakness, and the Japanese search for more secure economic outlets, the Manchurian invasion seemed to Japanese military and political leaders to be a natural step. As it turned out, the risk had been well calculated. The Soviet Union was caught in the midst of collectivisation and did little. The League proved unable to force one of its own members to renounce aggression, because it lacked the resources to do so other than moral pressure and the threat of economic sanctions. The latter were difficult to impose, not only because they excluded the United States, but because the major League powers were worried about the effect they would have on Asian trade and Far East security in general (**53**).

In 1933 Japan left the League and effectively removed the Far East from the system of collective security. In 1934, in violation of international agreements to preserve an 'Open Door' policy in China (to allow open and equal access to Chinese markets), the Japanese government announced the Amau Doctrine, a warning to other powers to regard China as Japan's sphere of influence and

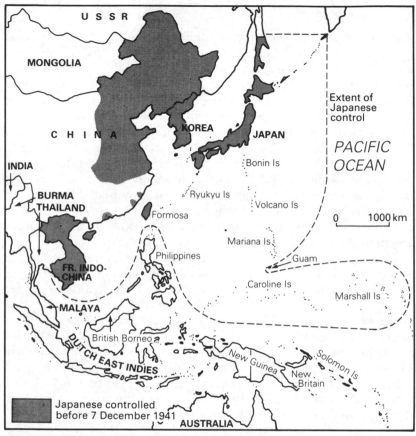

The Japanese empire by 1941

to abandon trade with the Chinese and the provision of technical aid to them. There is no doubt that Japanese leaders, spurred on at home by the military, were encouraged to go further after 1932 than they might otherwise have done because of the weak response from the major powers. Even the United States, architect of the 'Open Door' policy and naval limitations, hesitated to do anything that would alienate the Japanese. Neither Britain nor America was willing, in the difficult political climate of the early 1930s, to confront Japan militarily, and each suspected the other of trying to pass on the responsibility and cost of doing so (**82**).

The Manchurian crisis was critical in underlining the weakness of the League and the hollowness of the equilibrium which its supporters had established. It was followed by a sharp deterioration in the international situation in Europe. In January 1933 Hitler was appointed German Chancellor. He led a party committed to treaty revision and to a reassertion of German influence. From being a power that worked within the League system, however grudgingly, Germany now set out to repudiate it. Hitler withdrew the German delegation from the Disarmament Conference and the League of Nations in October 1933. The western powers already knew of German 'secret rearmament' before 1933 but had not perceived it as a serious threat. Under Hitler rearmament assumed a different character. Though the western powers had only a hazy idea of Hitler's ultimate intentions, it was clear that German rearmament would be directed at some time to a revision of the territorial settlement arranged at Versailles. This was not, as yet, a serious problem. The British, for their part, were not averse to some readjustment, provided it was achieved on British terms. But it did resurrect in a very direct way the threat that German power had posed to western interests before 1914. Britain and France were forced to look for ways in which Germany could be accommodated within the existing system without destroying its stability.

The rise of Hitler affected not only the western democracies but also Italy, where Fascism had come to power a decade before. Italy had been accommodated into League diplomacy. If Mussolini was still not taken quite seriously by western statesmen, he took himself seriously enough. Italy played a major part in the search for collective guarantees and by the early 1930s had acquired through dint of Mussolini's efforts a considerable increase in diplomatic stature and military strength. A powerful Germany threatened to undo some of these gains and to reduce Italian influence in central and south-eastern Europe. It is likely that this was the final factor that pushed Mussolini towards a policy of active imperialism in Africa and the beginning of an aggressive Mediterranean policy. Mussolini did not want to play the role of junior dictator to Hitler. As a result he brought Italy, in its turn, to a point where it could challenge the fragile balance of power.

Mussolini's imperialism had other roots as well, even though its emergence depended on diplomatic circumstances in Europe. Italian Fascism was preoccupied with ideas of an Italian mission to reconstruct the fallen Roman empire. This vision drew upon the pre-war anti-Slav and colonialist traditions, which helps to explain Mussolini's interest in the Balkans, and in east and north Africa.

He looked in particular at Ethiopia, the only major independent state left in Africa. Links with Ethiopia were of long standing. An agreement for friendship had been signed in 1928, and Italy's economic and military influence in the area had been tacitly acknowledged by the other major colonial powers, a fact that persuaded Mussolini that they would not object on grounds of principle to the extension of formal Italian control over the country. In September 1933 he made the first public announcement that Italy would be seeking an outlet in Africa and Asia. A war plan for the attack on Ethiopia was drawn up in the summmer of 1934 and in December he began active preparations for a campaign in the following autumn. In order to pre-empt possible retaliation from his League partners, Mussolini made efforts to create a favourable diplomatic situation which would ensure the success of his venture. In January 1935 he secured veiled agreement from the French Prime Minister, Pierre Laval. He hoped that Britain, too, would not be averse to Italian intervention, or could be restrained by France if she were, or would be frightened into acceptance by the military threat that Italy's Libyan armies posed to Egypt (**85, 105**).

In September 1935 Italian troops invaded Ethiopia. Though it was an unequal struggle, Italy's victory was hard won. It took over a year to conquer and pacify Ethiopia. Nor did Mussolini entirely succeed in his efforts to create diplomatic acceptance for his coup. The League rallied to Ethiopia's support, condemned the invasion, and talked fiercely of embargo and economic sanctions. But in practice the invasion of Ethiopia, like that of Manchuria, could not be reversed. France and Britain, as Mussolini had suspected, came close to giving some kind of approval to the Italian action, in the so-called Hoare-Laval Pact. Only the pressure of parliamentary and public opinion forced them to follow the League in condemning Italy. Economic sanctions broke down for the same reasons that had caused their failure against Japan. The United States and Germany could not be prevented from supplying goods, and the whole idea of sanctions challenged traditional free-trade attitudes, and might, it was feared, throw Italy into the arms of Germany. The self-interest of the major powers prevailed over the collective anxieties of the smaller nations of the League.

If Manchuria had begun the decline of the League system, Ethiopia brought about its eclipse. Sensing opportunities for gain, Japan and Italy tested the system to see what could be extracted.

Collective security evaporated, demonstrating the extent to which it had always rested on the willingness of Britain and France to enforce it. Instead, both the major western powers pursued their own interests, unwilling and unable to prevent a serious challenge to the stability and security of the international system. By 1939 the League strategy was bankrupt; confidence in the British and French claims to moral ascendancy in world affairs was, with some justice, at a low ebb. The Disarmament Conference, which the major powers had used as evidence of their good intentions, broke up without achievement in June 1934 and was not reconvened. The Ethiopian crisis opened up the way to rearmament and provoked the first murmurings of general war.

France and Britain

Britain and France were now faced with the question of how to respond to the deterioration in the international situation. There was never any doubt that some sort of response was called for. Neither power was prepared to abandon its influence, prestige and safety. Yet neither possessed sufficient strength, either military or economic, to assert that influence decisively when challenged. Both powers were confronted by the central dilemma of having to defend large and geographically dispersed empires with relatively shrinking resources. 'We are a very rich and very vulnerable Empire,' wrote Chamberlain, 'and there are plenty of poor adventurers not very far away who look upon us with hungry eyes' (**58**). Both British and French strategy was greatly complicated by the global nature of their concerns. Where Germany, Italy and Japan could concentrate their efforts at revision in geographically distinct regions, the two western powers were compelled to adopt a worldwide strategy.

It was only this shared threat that pushed Britain and France closer together in the 1930s. Certainly until 1933 Britain was wary of French ambitions, while the French were disappointed at the way in which Britain had withdrawn from direct involvement in Europe at the end of the war. There were other reasons for cool relations. Britain undermined French imperial interests in the Middle East and was not averse to some sort of colonial settlement with Germany. France, in turn, had proved unco-operative during the economic crisis and was held to bear much of the blame for the collapse of the international credit system in 1931. Chamberlain's private view was that France 'never can keep a secret for more than half an hour, nor a government for more than nine months' (**58**, p. 322). Until 1939 the British remained sceptical of France's value as an ally. The growing threat of Germany overcame some of these differences, but only on basic questions of the balance of power in Europe were there broad areas of agreement.

Yet even here the strategy that each adopted in the face of the German threat was very different. Both drew conclusions from the experience of 1914. The French, in the absence of an enforceable collective security, looked towards a system of firm alliances to restrain Germany. Britain wished to avoid at all costs the sort of alliance entanglements that were held to have brought about the First World War. Since France needed British support against Germany, the two strategies were clearly incompatible. In the end Britain was able to avoid any clear commitment to France until 1939, so that it was British strategy that tended to prevail, though France was never in any sense an entirely dependent or pliant instrument in British diplomacy.

French strategy was based on one major consideration: the need to find firm guarantees for security in the event of the revival of German power. Yet conditions for an alliance system were very different from those in 1914. Real guarantees for security could only be found in a formal military commitment to France by Britain, which was not forthcoming until February 1939. The other option was to work for a two-front containment of Germany. Following this strategy France established a network of alliances, some of them carrying military agreements are well, with the new states of eastern Europe. Agreement was reached with Poland in 1921, Czechoslovakia in 1924, Romania in 1926 and Yugoslavia in 1927. The so-called Little Entente in central Europe was intended to play the role that Russia had filled before 1914 (**39**). But such a relationship was fraught with problems. The promises of military aid were ambiguous, since France could clearly offer little immediate help in the event of a German thrust eastwards. Nor could the eastern states be relied on to agree among themselves sufficiently to restrain Germany with any effect. In 1935 France tried to secure a firmer base in the east by reaching an agreement with the Soviet Union, but this only served to alienate the smaller eastern powers from France while it provided no firm guarantee of any kind of Soviet action against Germany. To make things worse Belgium in 1936 overturned the military agreement of 1920 to co-operate with France, removing an important defensive line against Germany. Nor could Italy, once Mussolini had embarked on a Mediterranean strategy hostile to French interests, be used as a diplomatic make-weight to restrain German moves in central Europe, as had been hoped.

The French were finally compelled by circumstances to follow British strategy. The coming to power of the Popular Front of left-wing parties in 1936 made this easier, for it marked a shift away from support for the League and collective action, on which French foreign policy still formally rested, to a more active search for alternative ways of containing and accommodating German ambitions. British strategy was based on a clear conviction that firm alliances were a diplomatic liability and that all powers could be won over by adopting a flexible and pragmatic approach to problems as they arose. This conviction survived until 1939. Until then Britain avoided fixed commitments, particularly to France or to the countries of central and south-eastern Europe, while making spasmodic attempts to win over potential enemies by policies which the British regarded as realistic and reasonable. Third parties were used to bring pressure to bear, when needed, on other powers. Great weight was placed upon Britain's commitment to international morality. If such a strategy appeared to Britain's friends to border on incoherence, to Britain's leaders it resembled a gigantic and increasingly dangerous game of chess.

The key element in the game was to maintain what Chamberlain called a 'balance of risks'. Too firm a commitment in one part of the globe might disturb the balance in another. At all costs Britain had to avoid a simultaneous challenge in the areas of key strategic importance, in Europe, the Mediterranean and India. The Defence Requirements Committee report in 1935 summed up this principle: 'It is a cardinal requirement of our national and Imperial security that our foreign policy should be so conducted as to avoid the possible development of a situation in which we might be confronted simultaneously with the hostility of Japan in the Far East, Germany in the West and any power on the main line of communications between the two' (**89**, p. 176). When Chamberlain became Prime Minister in 1937 he adopted this principle as his own.

The word that British statesmen chose to describe this response was 'appeasement'. It was an unfortunate choice, for it came to imply a weak and fearful policy of concession to potential aggressors. In fact appeasement was far from that. It was more or less consistent with the main lines of British foreign policy going back into the nineteenth century. By appeasement was meant a. policy of adjustment and accommodation of conflicting interests broadly to conform with Britain's unique position in world affairs. It involved no preconceived plan of action, but rested on a number of political and moral assumptions about the virtue of compromise and peaceableness. It involved using the instruments of British power – trading and financial strength, and a wealth of diplomatic experience – to their fullest advantage. But it also implied that there were limits to British policy beyond which other powers should not be permitted to go. Appeasement was an acceptable strategy only as long as it matched what were perceived as British interests. Chamberlain saw himself as part of this tradition. When he became Prime Minister in June 1937 he assumed much more responsibility for foreign affairs than his predecessor, hoping to be able to produce a 'Grand Settlement' of international problems through a concert orchestrated by Britain.

Seen from the perspective of British foreign policy, the early reaction towards aggression and the breakdown of collective security make much more sense. Britain sought to treat problems as they arose, on their merits, but within certain loosely-defined parameters. In the Far East, for example, the British were prepared to accommodate Japanese ambitions, but only up to a point. It was recognised that Japan had a natural sphere of influence in northern China. It was hoped that Japan would counter the threat posed to India by the Soviet Union, and that she would become so embroiled in the problems of ruling Manchuria that she would no longer pose such a danger to peace. But acceptance of Japan's special position in the north was made only on the basis that Japan would respect the special privileges enjoyed by British trade and British officials throughout China (**82**). There were similar limits to Britain's appeasement of Italy. Some African and colonial readjustment was thought desirable throughout the 1930s. While condemning Italy at the League, Britain continued to search for ways of repartitioning Africa, possibly by using Portugal's colonies as bargaining counters. The Italian conquest of Ethiopia was not a vital concern to Britain, but the Italian threat to Egypt and Malta was. During 1936 and 1937 the British made efforts to drive a wedge between Hitler and Mussolini in the hope of making Italy more dependent on British and French goodwill. But at the same time both the western powers made it clear that continued Italian hostility was not to be tolerated and would be contained in Africa and in the Mediterranean in the absence of a reasonable settlement. The result was unfortunate in both cases, for appeasement pushed Italy and Japan closer to Germany (**101**).

With Germany the situation was altogether more delicate. Accommodation of German demands meant overturning the Versailles Settlement. This was less of a problem for Britain than for France. The British had been unhappy with the Treaty from the outset and had already made moves to conciliate Germany before Hitler came to power. The feeling was widespread that German grievances were, up to a point, justified, and that a lasting peace could only be secured by removing the more vindictive aspects of the peace settlement. Reparations were abandoned in 1931. Limited rearmament was tolerated. An Anglo-German Naval Agreement was signed in 1935. A return of German colonies, though not all, was contemplated [**doc. 2**]. None of this posed an immediate threat to British interests. The French were understandably much more anxious about making any concessions to Germany but were forced to accept the British approach because they could not contain Germany on their own.

Rightly or wrongly, British statesmen saw Germany as a power which, treated with respect and good sense, could be brought back into the great-power system without destroying it. There were plenty of warnings, from a wide variety of official and unofficial sources, that German ambitions were without limit, unpredictable and dangerous. With the benefit of hindsight we now know this to be true. But certainly until 1938 Hitler asked for nothing that the British were not, in the end, willing to grant. The British government was not prepared to give Germany a free hand in eastern Europe, or the right to tear up the Versailles Settlement on its own terms. Concessions to Germany were made in the knowledge that they fitted in with a realistic appraisal of British interests, even though they trampled on the interests of lesser powers. But they were made on what the British saw as their terms. Only when Hitler refused to accept this framework did the British state clearly, in 1939, the limits of their policy. Until then the British worked on the assumption expressed by Lord Halifax, that there was room for a 'possible alteration in the European order' (**91**, p. 29).

The problem was that appeasement, in order to be successful, had to be conducted from a position of some strength. Instead, the two western states found themselves offering concessions from a position of relative weakness. In the first place neither was sufficiently well-armed in the early 1930s to meet force with force without running the risk of weakening, perhaps fatally, its global interests. The pursuit of appeasement was therefore necessary to

19

buy time for rearmament. Then there were problems in domestic politics. There was strong pressure from pacifist opinion in both Britain and France to avoid any confrontation that might involve war. This pressure was underlined by the fear of bombing, shared by government and public alike. With the onset of air rearmament, governments everywhere were encouraged to be more circumspect in international affairs, not knowing, as we now do, that there were profound limitations of a technical kind which would have made it impossible for any power to launch a successful strategic bombing offensive in the 1930s (**45**).

There was also evidence of growing ideological conflict. British and French governments were more frightened of Communism than of Fascism in the mid-1930s. Certainly in Britain the traditional ruling class was not unsympathetic to Hitler and Mussolini, whereas they were deeply hostile to Communism. Sir Alexander Cadogan at the Foreign Office feared that 'war may place the whole of Europe at the mercy of Russia' (**19**, p. 84). This ambiguous assessment of Fascism explains the muted response of the western powers to the outbreak of civil war in Spain in 1936. 'In the present state of Europe,' argued the cabinet secretary, Sir Maurice Hankey, 'with France and Spain menaced by Bolshevism, it is not inconceivable that before long it might pay us to throw in our lot with Germany and Italy' (**91**, p. 39). Even by 1938 it was not clear exactly what sort of threat Fascism posed, but the threat presented by Communism had been made clear in October 1917. There were real doubts in conservative circles about whether or not the British and French working classes would support a more active foreign policy which might be interpreted as another 'capitalist war'. In France after the fall of the Popular Front some right-wing groups favoured closer collaboration with Hitler as the only way of preventing the eventual bolshevisation of western Europe.

America and Russia

All these factors – military weakness, fear of war, ideological and political conflict – had to be weighed in the balance when assessing foreign policy. They seemed to confirm the wisdom of adopting a conciliatory stand. But there were other, more imponderable elements in the international system which contributed to the general climate of uncertainty. This was particularly the case with the attitude of the United States and the Soviet Union to the growing international crisis.

United States foreign policy, according to Cordell Hull, Roosevelt's Secretary of State, could be summed up in one phrase: 'keeping this country out of war'. Americans had been deeply affected by the experience of intervention in the First World War. Throughout the inter-war years American governments avoided making commitments of any kind in Europe for fear that they would be dragged into conflict. This determination to avoid an active foreign policy was strengthened in the years of economic depression, when Roosevelt's economic recovery programme, the 'New Deal', took priority. Roosevelt hesitated to do anything abroad in case the powerful isolationist lobby undermined his domestic programme. To buy agreement at home the American government turned away from world affairs. Some isolationists wished to go even further than this. In 1935 they introduced a temporary Neutrality Act in Congress which became law in August, forbidding the granting of loans or the sale of arms to any belligerent. In January 1937 the act was extended to civil war in order to prevent the sale of arms to Spain, and on 1 May 1937 a permanent Neutrality Act was signed by Roosevelt which differed from the original act in that it allowed belligerents to fetch only non-war supplies from the United States in their own ships, for cash.

The strong desire for neutrality was matched by a general desire for appeasement [**doc. 3**]. American statesmen were convinced that the key to world peace lay in the recovery of the world economy. 'The truth is universally recognised,' said Hull, 'that trade between nations is the greatest peacemaker and civiliser within human experience.' A healthy economy would allow 'settlement among nations of any political questions' (**140**). Roosevelt played with the idea of a major conference to thrash all such questions out, which looked very much like Chamberlain's 'Grand Settlement'. But beyond vague pronouncements on the need for collective action and expressions of peace and goodwill, the American government did very little. In the Far East Japan was able to overturn the 'Open Door' with scant American resistance. When American ships were attacked by Japanese aircraft in China in December 1937 Roosevelt accepted a grudging Japanese apology but took no action. In Europe the United States, while clearly more sympathetic to the democracies than to the dictatorships, avoided open commitments. It was with deep regret that Roosevelt observed the gradual breakdown of the League system. Though he was willing to condemn aggression, as he did in his 'quarantine' speech on 5 October 1937, he remained committed to the idea that economic concessions and a deep respect for international morality were the necessary instruments for the proper conduct of world affairs (**56**).

The American attitude was also born of a deep distrust of British and French motives, which had taken root at Versailles when both powers scrambled for the imperial spoils from defeated Germany. American leaders could not rid themselves of the suspicion that Britain hoped to use American power, as in 1917, to rescue the Empire from collapse. In the Far East both powers played a complex game to avoid having to take the lead in confronting Japan. In November 1937 Roosevelt urged that America should not 'be pushed out in front as the leader in, or suggester of, future action' (**95**, p. 151). This view of Britain was confirmed by what Americans saw as Britain's unwillingness to make substantial efforts to restore free trade in her empire as a key to securing a more general economic settlement. American interests seemed more likely to be served by a general loosening of empire ties, a view that ran directly counter to the interests of the two major imperial powers. Britain, on the other hand, stood to gain a great deal from American support, yet could never be certain if any would be forthcoming. Chamberlain despaired of American foreign policy: 'It is always best and safest to count on *nothing* from the Americans except words' (**102**, p. 120). The neutrality legislation brought the prospect for Britain and France that it might encourage further acts of aggression by hostile powers. But attempts to lure the United States into underpinning western strategy failed at every turn before 1939. Nor, in the end, did Britain pursue such attempts with much determination, because of the danger that too great a dependence on the United States would reduce British influence and might involve substantial concessions on trade and colonial self-government. American help on these terms would be a very mixed blessing.

The same uncertainty and ambiguity characterised the attitude of the west to the Soviet Union. Russia's friendship, despite repeated assurances of her peaceful intentions, could not be counted on. In Soviet propaganda the British Empire was portrayed as the major enemy of the Soviet state. France had closer ties, and a greater interest in winning Soviet co-operation. But the pact signed in 1935 between the two countries was never effectively activated at a military level, and after the fall of the Popular Front and with the decline of the French economy, Russian leaders lost interest in French support. Russian strategy was similar to that of the United States: a strong desire to avoid war at all costs; a commitment to collective action for peace; and a strong suspicion that the western European powers merely regarded Russia as an instrument in their efforts to preserve world capitalism [**doc. 4**]. Like America, Russia wished to avoid any binding commitment. Though she had little confidence in the League of Nations, to which she was admitted in 1934, her Foreign Minister preferred it to a strategy of 'military alliance and the balance of power' which 'not only does not get rid of war, but on the contrary unleashes it' (**113**, p. 218). Formal, collective action through the League reduced the danger that Russia might be isolated by the capitalist powers. Soviet leaders rightly saw the greatest direct threat coming from Germany and Japan, but they did not as a result draw closer to Britain and France, partly from fear of alienating Germany and Japan still further, partly from a belief that the western powers were facing 'serious economic crisis' and could not be trusted to honour any bargain struck. Until 1939, when Russia found herself in the fortuitous position of being wooed by both sides, she kept out of the international arena. The European powers, for their part, while aware that Russia might at some stage play a vital part in the balance of power, believed that Stalin's industrialisation drive, and the savage purges that followed it, rendered Russia incapable of playing a full part in international affairs for the foreseeable future. Russian weakness, like American neutrality, made it harder to restrain Germany and Japan, though for the British and French it postponed the day when Communism might threaten the existing order (**113**).

From the Rhineland to Munich

American neutrality and Russian isolation did indeed carry the danger that Germany, Italy and Japan would be encouraged to pursue an adventurous foreign policy. So, too, did appeasement, which was interpreted not as great-power magnanimity but as a sign of weakness and moral decay. Once it became clear that the western powers would not take firm action, and indeed were willing to be conciliatory, the challenge to the existing system was rapidly extended. The three revisionist states were united in their rejection of the framework within which Anglo-French diplomacy was conducted. They saw mere arrogance in claims that could not be backed up by force. The slow pace of western rearmament and the constraints imposed by domestic political considerations appeared to show that here were empires in decline, decadent plutocracies whose course was run. Though they eschewed more formal alliances the three powers recognised their mutual interests in establishing a new diplomatic 'Axis'. In November 1936 Germany and Japan signed the Anti-Comintern Pact as a symbol of their desire for friendly co-operation. Italy joined the Pact a year later.

From 1936 onwards the international crisis could no longer be disguised. In March German troops reoccupied the Rhineland, demilitarized under the Versailles Settlement, while the powers were preoccupied with the Ethiopian affair. During the course of the year Germany accelerated the process of economic and political penetration into central and south-eastern Europe, withdrawing even further from the world economy and speeding up her rearmament. Italy followed the invasion of Ethiopia with intervention in the Spanish Civil War, where she was joined by German military personnel and equipment, fighting alongside the nationalist rebels. In 1937 Japan increased the pressure on the Chinese government at Nanking. When Chiang Kai-Shek finally rejected further Japanese encroachments, the Japanese army found a pretext for launching a full-scale war against China in November 1937. By January 1938 Nanking had fallen. By October Japan controlled the whole of northern and eastern China and threatened French, British and Dutch possessions in the Far East. In March 1938 Hitler seized a favourable diplomatic opportunity and occupied Austria, as he had intended since coming to power. During the course of the year the Nazi leaders turned towards Czechoslovakia, with its large German minority in the Sudetenland. Mussolini, though far from happy about the loss of Austrian independence, acted with mounting hostility towards the British and French throughout the Mediterranean basin. By early 1938 he had convinced himself that Britain was incapable any longer of checking the rise of Italian power and that by the spring of 1939 he would be well armed enough to defeat Britain and France without German help (**85**).

All this made appeasement look increasingly hollow. The international system was disintegrating. Warfare was now a permanent feature. For Britain and France the balance between conciliation and containment became increasingly strained. They were confronted with the stark paradox that the more they sought settlement and reconciliation, the more rapidly they created the conditions that made reconciliation impossible. Yet Chamberlain, for one, clung to the belief that appeasement, once properly understood, could still bring about international settlements on Britain's terms. After the German occupation of Austria, to which many British ministers had little objection in principle, the British turned their attention to the Czech crisis, to see whether it could be used as the means to bring about the general settlement they had been looking for.

During the spring and summer of 1938 the German leaders mounted a campaign of vilification against Czechoslovakia, the 'inconceivable creation' (Goering). While they publicly demanded that the German – speaking Sudetenland should be united with the new Reich they privately sought first the isolation and then the domination of the whole Czech state as a prelude to incorporating its economic resources with those of the Reich. The British and French governments took much the same view of the Sudeten problem. It was not an issue, remarked Cadogan, 'on which we should be on very strong ground for plunging Europe into war' (**91**, pp. 33–4). Though the French made more of their commitment to the Czechs, this was largely to appease domestic public opinion. It was not an issue on which the French Prime Minister, Edouard Daladier, was prepared to drag France into general war either. On 3 August 1938 the British sent an international delegation to the Sudeten areas, under Lord Runciman, to look at the possibilities of a peaceful settlement. Reasonable grounds were found for asking the Czech government to make concessions to Germany. Despite the fact that neither Russia nor France, both allied to Czechoslovakia, were willing or able to offer effective military help, the Czechs refused to comply. Fearing unilateral action on Hitler's part – Chamberlain thought him to be 'half-mad' – the British put pressure on the Czechs to capitulate. On 18 August the British succeeded in breaching Czech resistance, and on 22 August the French abandoned any pretence of upholding their treaty obligations to the Czechs. Chamberlain then negotiated directly with Hitler on the terms under which the Sudeten Germans would return to the Reich. When Mussolini invited the four major powers to meet at Munich on 28 September to determine formally the outcome of the Czech crisis, the fundamental agreements had already been reached. Russia was not invited, nominally on the grounds (given by Chamberlain) that the

Fascist leaders would refuse to sit down at a negotiating table with Soviet representatives, but in reality from the knowledge that Stalin would never agree to be a formal party to the dismemberment of Czechoslovakia. Germany was granted the Sudetenland in return for vague promises of future good behaviour [**doc. 5**]. Chamberlain conceded Germany's claim to economic influence in central and eastern Europe. Completely isolated diplomatically and under military threat from Germany, the Czech government had no alternative but to accept the terms of the Munich Pact. Britain offered a loan of £10 million to soften the blow. Chamberlain returned to Britain promising 'peace for our time'.

The Munich Pact was the high-water mark of Britain's strategy of appeasement. It was not a very moral agreement, for it abandoned the Czechs rather summarily to Nazi domination. But given the framework within which British diplomacy was forced to operate, it represented a realistic attempt by the Chamberlain government to assess Britain's vital interests and to balance those against the reality of western power. Though with hindsight we might conclude that something vital had been at stake in the Czech crisis, it was not immediately obvious in 1938. It seemed as if an element of stability might be restored to European affairs. The pact laid down the limited terms that Britain would accept for treaty revision in Europe, and it gave the appearance that Hitler had been compelled, like the Czech Prime Minister Benes, to accept the western powers as final arbiters in continental affairs. Hitler was no more anxious for general war in 1938 than the western powers. To avoid it he was forced to work for the last time, and with great reluctance, within the British framework. This fact alone excited within Chamberlain the prospect of achieving his general settlement. It opened up the chance of settling those economic and colonial issues which were thought to be the last stumbling blocks to agreement.

3   Economic and Imperial Rivalry

No single factor was more important in explaining the breakdown of the diplomatic system in the 1930s than the world economic crisis. What began as a slow fall in the business cycle in 1929 quickly accelerated into a recession of such intensity that unemployment rose to between one-fifth and one-third of the workforce in most of the industrial powers. The system of world trade and finance, already in difficulties during the 1920s because of war debts and a weak pound, collapsed. The volume of trade fell 70 per cent between 1929 and 1932. In 1931 Austria, and then Germany, came to the brink of national bankruptcy. Only a timely moratorium on all debts, initiated by the United States, prevented the world credit system from seizing up altogether.

The effects of the recession were immediate and far-reaching. The prices of foodstuffs and raw materials collapsed, leaving the poorer primary-producing countries and European and American farmers faced with a sharp fall in income, which in turn reduced demand for manufactured goods and pushed up unemployment and bankruptcies. In response governments sought ways of protecting their own producers and preserving trade at the expense of other countries. A deeply protectionist mood took root everywhere. American tariffs were sharply increased in 1930. France manipulated its currency to remain competitive abroad. Most alarming of all, Britain, the financial centre of the world market, finally abandoned the commitment to free trade and the gold standard and established a system of protection built around the empire. The investment that had flowed from London and Paris to oil the wheels of the world economy, already slowly declining during the 1920s, was reduced to a trickle after 1929, leaving smaller and weaker economies faced with serious currency and payments problems. This engendered a growing mood of resentment and disillusionment with the capitalist system in general, and with the more powerful industrial economies in particular (**77**).

Such resentment was expressed in the spread of ideas of self-sufficiency, or autarky. In order to avoid remaining at the mercy

27

of fluctuations in the world economy, it was argued that national economies should become as independent as possible of the world system, providing as much of their food and industrial requirements as they could with domestically-produced substitutes. This view was popular in the Fascist states, where economic independence was seen as desirable on nationalist grounds, and was first practised with mixed success in Mussolini's Italy. It was taken up as a major political objective after 1933 by the Nazi government, which blamed Germany's difficulties on foreign capitalists and bankers. Though it proved neither possible nor desirable to cut Germany off completely from the world economy, German trade remained at a low level and was closely controlled by the state, while foreign loans were excluded as far as possible. But if autarky was regarded in ideological terms as an expression of national economic virility, it was to some extent forced upon Italy and Germany by economic circumstances. Mussolini argued that the world was divided up into 'plutocratic' and 'proletarian' nations. Britain, France and the United States were very wealthy economies with vast material resources at their disposal. Germany, Italy and Japan were poor in natural resources, lacked great international wealth and were always in danger of being denied markets and raw materials by the 'plutocracies'.

The distinction between 'have' and 'have-not' nations, whatever its intellectual drawbacks, was a widely discussed and popular idea in the 1930s, and not only in Italy and Germany. It had its origins well before 1914 in arguments about the purpose of empire. Now, in the light of the economic slump, the idea was revived that there existed a demonstrable relationship between economic success and colonies, notwithstanding the awkward evidence that the most successful economy, the United States, was not an imperial power in any formal sense at all. The more Britain and France were forced to fall back on their empires for economic revival in the 1930s, the more forcefully the 'have-not' powers asserted their own right to empire. The world economic crisis thus had the effect of sharpening conflicts over markets and raw materials, undermining economic co-operation, and arousing once again dreams of imperial conquest.

The imperial powers

Imperialism did not disappear in 1918. When Britain and France took over German and Turkish colonies as mandates held on trust for the League of Nations, their empires reached their fullest extents. To the Far East and Africa were added territories throughout the Middle East. Over a quarter of the globe was ruled directly or indirectly by Britain, over one-third by Britain and France. It is important to realise the extent and size of British and French imperial interests, and the persistence with which they were upheld, if sense is to be made of western diplomacy in the years before the outbreak of war.

Empire was regarded by both powers as a vital interest. If at times it appeared a liability, no government (right or left) during the inter-war years was prepared to consider abandoning the imperial heritage or seriously questioned why Britain and France should have an empire at all. The mere possession of empire became justification enough. Without the empire Chamberlain thought Britain would be 'a fourth-rate power'. Empire was the source of Britain's greatness, the vehicle for the spread of French culture. French colonialists conjured up the vision of a new Mediterranean empire 'to extend the space occupied by our civilisation' and planned a great imperial railway from Paris across the Sahara desert to the Congo. The British now fully controlled the 'all-red route' from Britain to India. Gibraltar, Malta, Cyprus, Suez, Aden, Somaliland were all stepping stones to India, the centre-piece of the British Empire. That India should be defended was taken for granted. 'There will be no "lost dominion",' said Lord Birkenhead, 'until the moment – if ever it comes – when the whole British Empire with all that it means for civilisation, is splintered in doom' (**100**, p. 300). British prestige and world influence were so closely bound up with empire that there was never any serious doubt that Britain would fight to retain it. 'We have got most of the world already, or the best parts of it,' wrote Britain's First Sea Lord in 1934, 'and we only want to keep what we have got and prevent others from taking it away from us' (**101**, p. 3).

Above all, empire was assumed in an altogether uncritical way to be a source of economic advantage. On this ground the public at large could be persuaded that imperialism was in their interest as well, and did not stem purely from a desire for territorial aggrandisement and world power. In the aftermath of the 1929 slump, as British and French trade declined, the empires did indeed become relatively more important. France's investment in her empire rose from 9 per cent of her total overseas investment in 1914 to 45 per cent by 1940. Trade with the empire increased from 12 per cent of all French trade in 1929 to almost a third by

1936. The empire was a vital source of French supplies of rice, rubber, cocoa, coffee and valuable minerals (**41**). In Britain the economic connection became even more important. Exports to the empire rose from a third to almost half all British exports between 1910 and 1938. The amount of overseas investment from Britain going to the empire increased to 59 per cent of the total by 1929. Britain's Colonial Secretary talked in 1925 of Britain's tropical empire whose economic possibilities 'are perhaps greater than those available to us anywhere else in the world . . . immense territories, with immense natural resources' (**100**, p. 278).

Sentiments such as these served to reinforce the view abroad that British economic strength rested on her empire. Imperial protection was regarded by many as a natural expression of this special relationship in a world where free trade could no longer be practised with profit. Empire was presented to the electorate not as a moral mission but as a source of strength and advantage over other powers. Economic stability, and hence political stability, was said to hinge on empire. This in turn made the defence of empire, and fears for its safety, a central part of British foreign policy in the 1930s and a major factor in the pursuit first of appeasement, then of war.

In fact the advantage of empire was largely a delusion. Far from being a source of strength it was a growing liability, seriously undermining the capacity of both Britain and France to pursue their foreign policy goals, or to contain the aggressor powers. Imperialism strained relations between Britain and France at every turn, but especially in the Middle East, in Syria and Lebanon. The empires themselves were a constant source of friction and violence, with the spread of nationalism from Europe to the Third World and the growth of an educated native political class. For all the talk of unity, the British Empire was in the slow throes of disintegration. Ireland was lost in 1922. The Dominions were granted full autonomy in 1926. Years of nationalist struggle in India produced the Government of India Act in 1935 which paved the way for greater self-government. In 1936 the Anglo-Egyptian Treaty was signed which provided for greater parity between the two states and for joint control of the Suez Canal. South Africa, now dominated by those very same Boers that Britain had defeated in 1902, was increasingly hostile, while the other white dominions, although sympathetic to British needs, were far from firm in their support of the mother country (**57, 96**).

In many of the remaining parts of the dependent empire Britain was compelled to use force to prevent the erosion of her power. By 1939 a large part of Britain's military forces were on station in the Middle East. Political unrest was forcibly suppressed in Iraq, Egypt, Palestine and India. Nor was the French Empire any more secure. Civil war in the Middle East, Arab revolt in North Africa, and Communist agitation in Indo-China (where by 1932 there were 10,000 political prisoners) underlined the fragility of the empire. French colonial methods were harsh and inflexible. Throughout the empire high taxes, collective fines on villages, forced labour and summary execution were the price of French control. Its evidence in Syria proved too much even for the British, who forced the French to grant concessions. French colonialists were by and large still imbued with what the French Marshal Lyautey called 'the belief in inferior races whose destiny it is to be exploited' (**41**).

The British and French Empires failed to excite popular enthusiasm at home, except among those upper and middle-class groups whose livelihood and influence were dependent on colonies, and among the soldiers and politicians for whom empire had a visionary, sentimental appeal. The gains from imperial trade were offset by considerable liabilities. Protection was in the long run of more benefit to the Dominions than to Britain (**57**). India consumed more British resources than she returned. The military and administrative costs of empire were a constant source of concern to governments which, in more sober mood, became increasingly reluctant to bear the burden of empire. This was the great paradox of Franco-British strategy between the wars. Those same empires that were perceived to make Britain and France into world-class powers, the foundation of their security and strength abroad, were in practice a source of mounting insecurity and crisis. To defend them adequately required so great an expenditure of resources as to threaten the very stability the empires were supposed to provide. Yet failure to defend them was perceived as an end to British and French world power, which neither was prepared to accept.

The 'have-not' powers

The hard realities of imperialism did nothing to deflect the 'have-not' powers from their appetite for empires of their own. On the contrary, the weaknesses of the French and British empires were regarded as evidence that they were declining forces in world affairs, fit for overthrow by younger, more vigorous nations. Looking at the example set by Britain and France, the 'have-nots' assumed that territorial expansion and foreign rule were invariable features of the international system. As one empire fell, others arose to take its place. These ambitions were dressed up in the language of economic grievances and their just redress. All three 'have-not' powers, Germany, Italy and Japan, assumed that their long-term economic interests, indeed the very survival of their peoples, depended on the acquisition of large areas of conquered territory to be used as a source of materials and cheap labour and for the resettlement of surplus people from the home country. That much of this was in fact an illusion, since economic growth depended on a great many other variables, was never seriously considered. For in the end the quest for empire developed a momentum of its own, independent of economic ambition, a product of hazy notions of racial destiny and delusions of imperial grandeur borrowed from the west.

There was, of course, an element of truth in such arguments. The geopolitical circumstances of the Axis powers in the inter-war years did affect their economic performance and prospects for social stability. When compared with the richer states, Italy was short of almost all major industrial raw materials. So, too, was Japan until her conquest of China. Germany had lost a large part of her coal and iron deposits through the Versailles Settlement, and lacked secure sources of oil. Oil was particularly important as a vital strategic material for aircraft, ships and the new mechanised armies. Although all three powers could be supplied with it through normal trading channels, the sources of supply were easy for an enemy to intercept, and the arrangements for buying and shipping the oil difficult to operate. German and Italian supplies of iron ore were vulnerable on the same count. In the deteriorating conditions of world trade in the 1930s such fears seemed real enough.

Access to world markets and sources of capital was also fraught with difficulties. Japan found herself progressively excluded from Asian and African markets by British and French protective measures aimed largely at Japanese goods. German trade and investment were replaced in central Europe and the Balkans by those of Britain and France after 1919. Other forms of discrimination were introduced. Italian emigration to the United States was restricted after the First World War; Japanese emigration to Australia and America was closed off by the 1930s. The populations of both countries continued to grow at a high rate, a fact that exacerbated the impact of unemployment and low incomes in the years of world recession. No doubt Japan, Germany and Italy were inclined to grumble more than was necessary. Their economies experienced relatively high rates of growth during the 1920s. Nor were the protectionist measures taken by the western powers the product of deliberate malice, but more of economic self-interest (and to some extent as a retaliation against protectionism in the 'have-not' nations themselves). What mattered was that the slowing down in economic and trade growth and the spread of protectionism were perceived by political forces in the three countries as a deliberate attempt to restrict and inhibit the natural expansion of the new economies.

It was thus the *political* hostility that economic rivalry produced which mattered. Expression was given to this hostility not only through the ambitions of the dictators themselves, but through the economic and imperial demands of political parties – the Fascists in Italy, the Nazis in Germany – and through the expansionist demands of the armed forces. The economic complaints became subsumed in less rational arguments about the necessity for military and territorial expansion. While it would be wrong to maintain that there existed a coherent and pre-planned timetable for war, it is impossible to ignore the powerful evidence that war and conquest became major ambitions in all three states during the 1930s. Pushed on by economic circumstances and the pressure of political nationalism at home, all three powers sought to redress the balance of world affairs in their own favour.

Japanese expansion did not begin with the invasion of Manchuria, but with the occupation of Korea in 1894. During the First World War and the 1920s piecemeal expansion continued. Arguably in the Japanese case the pressure to go further than this and occupy Manchuria was based on a fear of Russia and China and the search for an effective buffer state, as Japanese leaders claimed. But this is to ignore the steady pressure to extend Japanese power throughout the western Pacific seaboard, and the continued encroachment on Chinese sovereignty from Manchuria, once it had been occupied. Nor does it adequately explain the colonial character of Japanese rule in Korea and Manchuria, whose economies and labour force were made to conform with Japanese requirements on unfavourable terms. Nevertheless, Japanese civilian politicians, though committed to the extension of Japanese power, were more opportunistic and cautious in their diplomacy than their military colleagues. Not until the army revolt of 1936 did pressure grow at home to extend Japanese influence throughout eastern Asia. The failure of the other major Pacific powers to restrain Japan encouraged greater risk-taking as well. In 1938 Japan sought to give its expansion more coherence by establishing an Asian 'New Order' based upon Japanese military and economic hegemony in northern and eastern China, and cultural and diplomatic pressure elsewhere [**doc. 6**]. This laid the foundation for the so-called 'Co-Prosperity Sphere' set up during the war, which stretched from Manchuria in the north to Burma and the Dutch East Indies in the south. At no point in this expansion were Japanese leaders prepared to abandon any of their conquests. They ignored the Brussels Conference called in November 1937 by Roosevelt to discuss the future of China, and actively sought to extend their influence into the colonial areas of the Far East (**74, 82**).

Italian expansion too was carried out within areas of historic Italian concern: in North and East Africa, on the Dalmatian coast, and the islands of the Mediterranean. Mussolini blended together old-fashioned colonialism and Fascist ideology. 'Fascism', it has been said, 'lived on dreams of future prosperity' (**85**, p. 107). Empire was pursued in order to make the Italian people wealthy, but it was also to give them a sense of racial superiority. Only through recreating the old Roman Empire in the Mediterranean and Near East, argued Mussolini, could Fascism provide full expression for the vigorous leadership and the harsh, heroic values of the movement. Brought up on propaganda and rhetoric about the glories of Mussolini's new Italy, Italians needed somewhere to rule [**doc. 7**]. Mussolini actively built up the Italian armed forces to a point at which he believed Italy strong enough to begin its civilising mission. As opportunities presented themselves, this crude vision of empire was gradually adopted as Italian national policy. Ethiopia was the corner-stone of this new imperialism. Fascist writers argued that it was rich in raw materials and would become the industrial heartland of Africa. Vast areas for the settlement of Italian emigrants were seized from Ethiopian owners. Libya was to be developed in the same way. In all the Italian conquests colonial government was introduced. Racial laws were enacted to prevent miscegenation. Colonial governors were instructed not to see the colonies as areas being slowly nursed to self-government, but as areas ripe only for domination by a superior culture (**85**).

Sooner or later, Mussolini realised, he would have to confront Britain and France in both Africa and the Mediterranean. Because neither power had opposed the conquest of Ethiopia by force, nor Italy's intervention in Spain, Mussolini came to assume that it was only a matter of time before he could replace them as the major power in the region. In 1939 Italian troops occupied Albania, threatening Yugoslavia to the north and Greece to the south, but also threatening Britain's vital interests in the Middle East. Italy now had, according to her ambassador in London, Dino Grandi, 'complete dominion over the eastern Mediterranean'. There was a good deal of delusion and wishful thinking in Fascist policy. It is hard to judge the extent to which Mussolini was a serious imperialist, or had simply become the victim of his own propaganda and the necessity of keeping Fascism on the boil. Either way there was no going back. War, he claimed, was 'the normal condition of peoples and the logical aim of any dictatorship' (**85**).

German ambitions differed in a number of important respects from those of Italy and Japan. The latter powers were concerned chiefly with the establishment of a geographically defined hegemony, the one in the Mediterranean basin, the other in east Asia. Under Hitler, Germany sought world power. Traditional German expansionism had looked mainly to central and eastern Europe as a 'natural' area of German influence. Overseas colonies were never as important as they were to the western powers, though German conservatives would have liked to have them back after Versailles. But Hitler's vision of empire transcended the traditional aims of German foreign policy. It was a vision far more coherent and consistent than that of Italy and Japan. Though it was shared widely with other leaders of the Nazi party, it derived its strength and scope from Hitler alone. The concept of empire was central to National Socialist ideology. It grew out of Hitler's ideas on the historical necessity of struggle between different races and cultures, and his belief that alone among nations only Germans and Jews seriously contested for world-historical power. Hence if Germany were to fulfil its true historic mission the other great powers, which Hitler came to regard as degenerate, had to be pushed aside and world Jewry annihilated in the process (**124, 131**).

These were not mere dreams, though they may have seemed so when Hitler wrote them down in *Mein Kampf* in 1924. Once in power they formed the loose framework for the conduct of foreign policy and domestic affairs. Specific plans were gradually unfolded as Hitler consolidated his political position at home. Many

35

Germans, and not just Nazis, welcomed the remilitarisation of Germany. They supported too the efforts to revise the Versailles Treaty. But for Hitler this was a mere beginning, while the foundations were laid for massive warfare in the future and the German people were psychologically prepared for the experience of total war. German empire was to be acquired in two complementary stages [**doc. 8**]. In the first stage Germany was to establish without general war the old idea of *Mitteleuropa*, a central and eastern European area dominated by Germany which could be used to provide the material resources (coal, iron ore, labour, oil) necessary for the prosecution of the next stage. This initial stage called for union with Austria, the incorporation of Czechoslovakia, the domination or incorporation of western Poland, and the economic and diplomatic subordination of Hungary and the Balkan states. During 1936 and 1937 these aims were made known to the military and party leaders. How they were to be achieved depended to some extent on the pace of rearmament and the opportunities offered by diplomatic circumstances. But there is no doubt that Hitler had by this stage both a plan and a rough timetable. Once German domination in eastern Europe was an accomplished fact, Germany was to develop vast new industrial resources as a springboard for the next and major stage of German expansion, the winning of living-space (*Lebensraum*) in the east.

The conquest of western Russia was a vital part of Hitler's plan for expansion. It opened up the prospect of threatening India, and driving the British and French from the Middle East. If neither western power was prepared to accept domination by Germany on Hitler's terms, then they, too, would be defeated and the colonial empires torn up. Behind the western powers lay the United States, symbol for Hitler of racial degeneration. At some unspecified time in the future would come a final reckoning with America for world dominion. Hitler ordered Albert Speer, the party architect, to schedule the completion of the gigantic Berlin victory buildings for 1951.

All this required a massive military effort and an unyielding commitment to war. 'All the time my thoughts are circling round one thing,' Goering told economic leaders in 1938, 'when will war come? Shall we win? What can we do? . . . only a nation that stakes everything on its armaments will be able to continue its existence' (**98**, p. 78). War for Hitler was a historical and racial necessity. Whatever its cost to the German people, even if it meant the eventual destruction of Germany, it was impossible to shirk the final test. Was all this mere fantasy conjured up in the days of Hitler's political adolescence, or a version of the Fascist rhetoric displayed in Italy? Neither seems likely. Despite their fantastic and irrational character, there can be no doubt that Hitler's convictions were held with an almost Messianic intensity, and that he meant, if he could, to put them into practice. Because the political system constructed in the Third Reich depended so centrally on Hitler, he was freed from many of the normal constraints on foreign policy. His vision became, willy-nilly, the vision of Germany.

There was, nevertheless, as in France and Britain, a considerable gap between dream and reality for all three powers. Disagreement existed among the ruling élites over the conduct of foreign policy, particularly in Japan where some civilian ministers thought the risk of confronting Britain and the United States too high. In Italy imperialism was compromised by incompetence and corruption, and by the evident reluctance of the Italian people to assume the imperial role assigned to them by Mussolini. Few colonists could be found to take up the offer of land in Libya and Ethiopia, and those who did found themselves the victims of corrupt regional officials. The Italian military also felt a profound apprehension at the prospect of war, a fact to which Mussolini remained impervious. Even in Germany the conduct of foreign policy was conditioned at first by a necessary circumspection. German soldiers who entered the Rhineland in March 1936 had orders not to shoot if opposed by French or British troops. Yet with the success of each initiative, confidence grew in all three countries about the prospects for further expansion, narrowing down policy choices more rigidly in favour of war. Gradually foreign policy moved from the diplomacy of opportunity to the diplomacy of intention.

The failure of 'Economic Appeasement'

Much of the economic argument of the 'have-not' powers was understood in the west. The American Secretary of State thought that the rise of political nationalism was the 'characteristic expression of great people in revolt against the limitations placed upon their national prosperity by their poverty in natural resources'. Restoration of free trade and international prosperity would reduce the threat of war: 'discontent will fade and dictators will not have to brandish the sword and appeal to patriotism to stay in power' (**140**, p. 89). Chamberlain shared this commercial view of world affairs: 'Might not a great improvement in

Germany's economic situation result in her becoming quieter and less interested in political adventures?' he asked Halifax (**101**, p. 138). There was an underlying assumption that Germany and Japan did have real economic claims which had to be respected, and that economic concessions in these areas would go far to eliminating the evident sense of grievance that both powers harboured towards the west.

This was the origin of economic appeasement. Beginning in 1936 the western powers sought to find terms on which the 'have-not' powers could be brought back fully into the world economy as a prelude to a general, and peaceful, settlement of outstanding political differences [**doc. 9**]. The real barrier to agreement was protection and exchange control, which blocked up the arteries of world trade and undermined prospects for a return to the more stable world economy of the 1920s. Some preliminary agreements were reached in 1934 between Britain and Germany on trade and payments. Fitful discussions took place between the heads of industry in both countries. Some rearrangement of eastern European trade was achieved in 1938. An agreement on coal exports was reached in January 1939. With Japan no satisfactory agreement could be reached. Britain also held out the prospect of a return of some German colonies as a sign of goodwill, to be accompanied by a substantial loan to Germany to ease what were assumed to be substantial trade and capital difficulties there. It was hoped that the promise of economic redress would persuade the more moderate elements in the German government to bring influence to bear on Hitler to take a more reasonable course and end the policy of autarky (**118**).

In practice economic appeasement was no more successful than diplomacy in accommodating Germany and Japan within the western system. There were a number of reasons for this. First of all the western powers were unable to agree among themselves about economic reconstruction. The stabilisation of the international currency system in 1936 was the only major agreement between them. In 1938 the van Zeeland report drawn up by a League of Nations committee called for full international economic co-operation, but it was not acted upon. Britain was reluctant to make major concessions on imperial protection, which was the price America wanted for fuller economic co-operation. The economic recession in 1938 revived fears of another collapse like that of 1929 and temporarily pushed the powers back towards policies of self-interest. Most important of all, Italy, Germany and Japan were distrustful of western motives. Goering thought that more German exports would only serve to bolster western rearmament at Germany's expense. Far from being the 'moderate' that the west hoped, Goering was at the head of those groups in Germany transforming the economy to large-scale war preparations. The real moderates around Schacht were largely without political influence inside Germany. Nor were economic conditions there as poor as Britain thought; or at least not poor enough to throw Germany into the arms of her richer neighbours.

Though Chamberlain hoped that economic appeasement would produce diplomatic dividends, and did so right up until the outbreak of war, he also argued that Britain should use its considerable economic power as a weapon to contain the aggressor states: 'The idea was that we should use our financial strength and resources for political purposes' (**91**, p. 42). The outcome was a sharp acceleration in economic rivalry from the mid-1930s onwards, particularly in the Balkans and Middle East, in Latin America and in China, which occurred simultaneously with continued efforts at economic conciliation.

The situation in the Balkans and central Europe demonstrated this ambiguity. The region had long been regarded in the west as an area where Germany might pursue legitimate trading interests. During the German economic recovery after 1933 trade in the area was slowly built up on the basis of special treaties and bilateral payments agreements. Eastern European states bought manufactured goods and arms from Germany in return for raw materials and food which they could not sell easily in the west. British and French influence, particularly in Poland, Czechoslovakia and Hungary, declined relative to that of Germany. By 1938 Germany provided an average of 29 per cent of the exports of the countries of eastern and south-eastern Europe, and 29 per cent of their imports. Britain and France provided only 13.5 per cent and 11.2 per cent of exports and imports between them. Britain's reaction was to welcome German initiatives to the extent that they stabilised the area (particularly against the Russian threat), but to deplore the collapse of freer trade in the area at her own expense [**doc. 10**]. In the discussions leading up to Munich a rough agreement was worked out dividing eastern Europe into different spheres of economic influence. Britain and France, both of which had begun to withdraw economically from central Europe even before the Munich Pact, conceded this area to Germany in return for an understanding that they should be able to continue their economic activity in the Balkans and Turkey (**75**).

It was here that Britain and France were determined, if they could, to limit German expansion. Both states hoped to use their economic strength to hold up German economic penetration southwards. Turkey was regarded as vital in this respect, and was granted a credit of £16 million in May 1938 to secure her support. Greece and Romania were likewise promised financial aid and the prospect of more exports to the west during 1939 as part of a general, though rather ineffectual, strategy of containment. Compared with the British promise to buy limited quantities of Romanian wheat and Greek tobacco, the German negotiators offered a much more comprehensive package of loans, export agreements and arms. A long-term Romanian-German Trade Treaty was signed in March 1939. Generous trade credits were extended to Yugoslavia and loans negotiated in the autumn of 1938 with Turkey and Bulgaria. During 1939 British and French capital was progressively excluded from eastern Europe. The smaller Balkan countries, though anxious for more help from the west, were drawn further into the German net.

Similar rivalry sprang up in China and Latin America. In both areas America's 'Open Door' policy was repudiated. Germany made agreements similar to those made in the Balkans with the countries of Latin America. Japan sought to exclude western influence from northern China altogether and to dictate the terms on which loans and goods could be sent to the south. In both areas the response of the United States, though couched in the language of economic appeasement, was less compromising than the western response in the Balkans. In China American aid helped to stabilise the Chinese currency, while American loans (despite the Neutrality Act) sustained Chinese resistance to Japan. In their approach to Germany American statesmen argued in favour of economic pressure through a comprehensive trade agreement programme which, it was claimed, was 'a ready forged weapon in hand to induce Germany to meet world trade and political settlement' (**89**, p. 393). When Germany refused to respond on American terms, economic conflict was intensified.

Did this mean that the war was in the end caused by economic rivalry? It was widely held in left-wing circles in the 1930s that wars were caused by capitalism. There is little direct evidence to support this view now. Businessmen in all countries favoured peace and the maintenance of international stability as a key to expanding trade and profits. In Germany, Italy and Japan many of the leaders of heavy industry and export industries were distrustful of extreme nationalism and the growing role of the state in economic affairs. Contacts were established between American, French, British and German industrialists, notably in chemicals and iron and steel, to reach international agreements on trade and output. Discussions between German and British businessmen continued into the summer of 1939. Of course, as we have seen, economic competition survived and indeed was strengthened during the 1930s, but it was not itself the cause of war. Had the aggressor powers simply been concerned with trade and raw materials, then they might well have been satisfied with economic concessions from the west. But Hitler and Mussolini and the Japanese nationalists could not be bought off. To them economic conflict had a basic political cause, the unequal distribtion of territory and political power. They politicised economic rivalry and expressed it in terms of a quest for empire. Economic settlement would only be possible once the political conflict was resolved.

Even Chamberlain, who more than anyone remained convinced that the dictators could be bought off by promises of economic gain, lamented in 1938 that 'Politics in international affairs governs actions at the expense of economics, and often of reason' (**27**, p. 247). If the war had a capitalist character at all, it was far more the case for Britain and France, where it was believed in governing circles that the international political crisis was directly caused by economic difficulties, and that the major threat posed to western interests was to their trade and financial influence, which in turn brought into question economic stability and political security at home. But even in Britain and France this problem was expressed not in crude economic terms (which would have been less popular at home) but in terms of empire and ideology. The war was fought in the end as a contest for political power, the culmination of that long and unstable period of empire-building which had begun in the middle of the nineteenth century.

4 Armaments and Domestic Politics

The contest for imperial and economic power could only be met by a great increase in military strength. Cadogan might well have spoken for all the powers when he told Chamberlain that 're-armament is a vitally necessary first step' without which 'it is difficult to have or to pursue a foreign policy' (**91**, p. 58). The level of armed strength crucially determined the willingness of the powers to risk war, and eventually the timing of war itself. During the 1920s limited disarmament was adopted by the major powers, not on grounds of international morality alone, but because no immediate military threat appeared on the international horizon. A higher level of military preparedness – especially for Britain and France, still the most heavily armed powers in the 1920s – would have been an unnecessary expenditure of industrial and human effort. During the depression military spending continued to fall. The Disarmament Conference, in session at Geneva between 1932 and 1934, called for serious efforts at multilateral reduction of arms as a prelude to the dawn of a new age of peace and plenty. The conference was soon overtaken by events. Growing international instability provoked the onset of worldwide rearmament.

Rearmament

Rearmament was not confined to Germany and the western powers. Japan and Italy continued to arm throughout the depression years, and Russia under Stalin embarked in 1929 on a series of Five-Year Plans part of whose object was the massive militarisation of the Soviet Union in the face of the threat from the 'capitalist powers'. A great many lesser powers, China, Czechoslovakia, Poland, Spain and Turkey, pursued the same course. The League of Nations calculated that world military expenditure increased from $3.5 thousand million in 1925 to $5 thousand million in 1934. This increase was fuelled partly by distrust of the willingness or the ability of the League to enforce collective security; and partly by the desire of emergent nations to build up their own armed forces as a sign of national maturity, a vanity that the major arms producers were only too ready to satisfy. Trade in armaments increased sharply during the 1930s, from $34 million in 1932 to $60 million in 1937.

The German military threat really developed too late to be the main cause of this rearmament. Britain was more concerned with Japan, and France with Italy until 1935. But once the German threat became clearer, it encouraged the onset of a specific arms race between the three western powers which took place against the general background of world rearmament. This was inevitable once they identified Germany as the major threat to peace. Germany was committed to large-scale rearmament, though not directed solely against the west. Britain and France used what they knew of German war preparations as a rough yardstick for their own military expenditure and arms plans.

All three powers believed that the next war, if it came, would be a total war; a long war that required the mobilisation of the nation's entire military and moral resources. This was to some extent a natural reaction to the war of 1914, which the powers had expected to be 'over by Christmas', but which had lasted instead for four years. German generals analysed the nature of *totaler Krieg*, 'total war'. French strategists talked of '*La guerre de longue durée*'. British strategy, with its central emphasis on naval power and financial strength, was always more committed to tactics of attrition than to short and decisive land campaigns. For Hitler the idea of a total war fitted in with his dreams of racial struggles of titanic proportions, of the final reckoning between the powers.

There were also very practical reasons for expecting a long war. The military leaders of the 1930s had all been through the experience of the First World War. Though a growing body of opinion among younger officers in all three countries favoured ideas of the quick, mobile campaign, the main weight of military thinking was still expressed in terms of the western front: the machine gun, the artillery barrage, defence in depth by armies of huge size. The French Maginot Line, a long system of fortifications which resembled a heavily armed concrete 'trench', was built along the whole French border with Germany. The German military later built similar fortifications, the 'Westwall', on their side of the Rhine. The First World War also demonstrated the increasing industrialisation of warfare. The armed forces had to be supplied with huge quantities of advanced military equipment, which required a total mobilisation of industrial and labour resources at home.

The threat of blockade by the western powers, which the German army blamed for its eventual capitulation in 1918, gave added impetus to ideas about mobilising the home front in Germany. The German army planned in the 1930s a comprehensive system of total mobilisation which they called *Wehrwirtschaft* – the defence economy. French and British soldiers shared much of this view. In any future war victory would go only to the countries that produced the most military equipment. Since the full mobilisation of such resources took time, the war would be a long-drawn out affair, a test of endurance.

Preparation for such a conflict was a problem of enormous complexity. Much rearmament was a question of intelligent guesswork, but guesswork nonetheless. The scale of military preparations and the timing of production plans depended not only on the domestic resources available, but upon intelligence of what other powers were planning to produce. Additionally, account had to be taken of the rapid changes in military technology. Over the course of the 1930s the quality and performance of major weapons, particularly aircraft, altered dramatically. Wood and canvas biplanes gave way to all-metal single-wing aircraft of much higher performance. Radio and radar transformed military communications. By 1939 jet aircraft, rockets, even nuclear weapons, were in the early stages of development. Another crucial variable was a proper estimate of the number and character of potential enemies. For some powers this was much easier to calculate than for others. Japan and Italy, whose foreign policy depended to a great extent on winning local advantage over powers which were otherwise much stronger, concentrated on naval rearmament and fighter-bomber aircraft sufficient to achieve local superiority. The three major powers, Britain, Germany and France, had to be prepared for every contingency.

German rearmament had begun in a very limited way before 1933. In February 1933 Hitler announced, amid general approval from the heads of the armed forces, a long-term plan for German military build-up. But the first priority was to restore the infrastructure of military life, the barracks, airfields, fortifications and installations, that Germany had been denied under the conditions of the Versailles Treaty. This also meant a vast training programme to catch up with the other powers in the number of trained men and officers. Up to 1937 over 50 per cent of all German aircraft produced were trainers (**133**). Much of the military expenditure undertaken before 1939 went on buildings rather than the production of weapons. At the same time the armed forces, and the army in particular, set about planning for the economic co-ordination of the nation's resources should war eventually break out, a policy they christened 'armament in depth' instead of 'armament in width'. A special Plenipotentiary for War Economy was appointed in 1935. Every part of Germany belonged to a 'defence area' with its own armaments and economic staff who organised the mobilisation of local economic resources (**51**).

The effect of all this basic preparation was to reduce the proportion of military spending that Germany could actually devote to weapons and equipment, though rearmament was pursued so conspicuously and with such energy that foreign observers came away with the impression that Germany possessed large-scale and well-equipped armed forces sooner than was actually the case. In fact by 1936 German rearmament had reached something of a crisis point. Though the armed forces were happy to go on expanding until Germany had been restored to what they saw as her rightful weight in European affairs, the civilian ministers, led by the Minister of Economics, Hjalmar Schacht, were unhappy about the escalating cost of rearmament in a country slowly dragging itself out of the worst depression in its history. Hitler, however, had no reservations. In September 1936 he appointed Goering to head the new Four-Year Plan which was to be the foundation of Germany's preparation for total war [**doc. 11**]. Goering acquired the responsibility in the years 1936–38 for the whole of German economic life, and with his circle of officials and appointees greatly increased state control over the economy in order to push rearmament on faster (**141**). In 1938–39 rearmament expenditure rose by 70 per cent above the level of the previous two years. The armed forces began to draw back, partly from fear of the effects excessive rearmament would have on the German economy, partly from a growing uncertainty about what Hitler was really preparing for.

But by now it was too late. Hitler was committed to a war of 'great proportions'. A large programme for the production of synthetic strategic materials was set in motion. Hitler activated a new naval building programme in January 1939 to give Germany a great battle fleet once again. He ordered a quintupling of air force strength, including a strategic bomber force, and laid the foundations for an army with a large mechanised core. The end date for these preparations was fixed for the mid-1940s, when Germany would be ready to fight the great powers. In 1938 and

1939 this process was far from complete. There were no firm military plans for campaigns either to east or west, nothing to compare with the Schlieffen Plan of 1914. In order to mask the longer time-scale of German preparations Hitler pursued a policy of putting as much as possible in the 'shop window' to give the impression that Germany was armed in greater depth than was in fact the case (**54, 134**).

French strategy, as we have seen, was based on the same expectation of a great war. French military thinkers argued that given France's likely resource deficiencies in the early stages of any war, it was necessary to plan a war in two stages. The first stage should be purely defensive, preventing the enemy from reaching French soil. In the late 1920s, under the inspiration of General Maginot, a defensive line was built incorporating massive fire-power of artillery and machine guns, which was designed to make France inpenetrable. The second stage was the building up of an offensive striking power, including heavy bombers, so great that it could eventually break out from the defensive line and overwhelm the German army by sheer volume of military material. Marshal Pétain argued that France could eventually produce twelve times as much equipment as the Germans, because of the effects of blockade on the German economy and the superior financial strength of France in world markets (**146, 147**).

The strategy of the total use of economic resources was accepted by French civilian and military leaders alike. But as in Germany it was difficult to get agreement about the level or pace of rearmament. French decisions had to be taken against a background of deteriorating economic conditions and growing political conflict between right and left. By 1937 French aircraft production was only a third that of Britain, one-eighth that of Germany. Overall military expenditure stagnated: 14 billion francs in 1932, and only 15 billion francs in 1936. Even this effort met resistance in French political circles because of the threat it posed to domestic stability at a time when capital was flooding out of France to escape the policies of the Popular Front. This slow expansion was less damaging to French interests than it appeared, however, since France had been until the mid-1930s the foremost military power in Europe and was still left with an important foundation on which to build. By 1939 military expenditure had increased sixfold over 1936. In tank and aviation technology France was at least the equal of Germany. Though there was ground to make up, it would be wrong to exaggerate the degree to which France was materially unprepared at the outbreak of war (**60**).

There were strong similarities in British strategic planning, though the pace of British rearmament was faster. Britain, like France, placed great emphasis on the need for effective defence. But Britain also hoped to build up sufficient armed force to act as a deterrent to other powers, making offensive action unnecessary: 'The fear of force is the only remedy,' thought Chamberlain (**58**, p. 252). It was this that held Britain back from making any firm continental commitment before 1939. Rearmament was geared to British strengths rather than weaknesses. Britain lacked a large continental army because she had very different strategic priorities from Germany and France. Instead Britain hoped to use her economic strength and the traditional strategy of blockade and attrition to contain Germany in the event of war, while building up an active air defence at home to prevent bombing and invasion. Economic power was regarded in this respect as vital. Like the French, British leaders were convinced that great financial and commercial strength offset the lead that Germany might enjoy in military material. It was, argued Inskip, Minister for the Co-ordination of Defence, an essential element in Britain's defensive power, 'one which can properly be regarded as a fourth arm of defence, alongside the three Defence Services, without which purely military effort would be of no avail' (**101**, pp. 102–3). Naval power was also a vital concern. It was only through naval rearmament that effective defence could be established of the route to India and of Britain's Far Eastern empire. The navy was one of the key instruments in the pursuit of an effective blockade of potential enemy powers, particularly Germany. Economic warfare could also be conducted from the air, through bombing attacks on an enemy's industry and the morale of his workforce. For that purpose, but with variable enthusiasm, the government supported the Royal Air Force in its efforts to build up a bomber striking-force during the 1930s. The great advantage of strategic bombing, as it was called, was thought to lie in the fact that Britain could bring the war to the European mainland from British bases without the need to commit large armies to a continental campaign. Indeed some air strategists hoped that bombing on its own, through the attrition of enemy economic capacity, might act decisively to bring the war to an end.

All of these were long-war strategies, requiring the careful husbanding of resources and considerable planning for economic mobilisation. Serious consideration of these long-term questions began in 1935 with the influential Defence Requirements Committee, first set up in November 1933. In March 1936 its conclusions formed the basis of a four-year plan for rearmament. Priority went to air force and naval expenditure and funds were 'rationed' on this basis. Expenditure increased from £185 million in 1936 to £719 million in 1939. There were plenty of critics who argued that not enough was being spent, or that the government's priorities were the wrong ones, particularly in the army, which was frustrated in its efforts to get army armaments any sort of priority. Certainly Baldwin and Chamberlain hoped initially that rearmament could be undertaken on the basis of a limited commitment which would not strain British resources too greatly, nor threaten political stability. But in 1937, when Chamberlain became Prime Minister, caution was thrown to the winds. Chamberlain ordered a full inquiry into the scope and purpose of Britain's rearmament plans. Together with the military leadership, he decided that Britain should prepare for total mobilisation. As in France, a great armament effort was scheduled for 1938–40.

The Treasury, with some reluctance, released ever greater funds to meet the services' demands. Air plans were hurriedly revised upwards. Construction of the great naval base at Singapore was speeded up. Mobilisation plans were drawn up for the total utilisation of Britain's economic and manpower resources. A defensive skeleton was built up between 1936 and 1939 which was to be fleshed out once war had actually started. In late 1938 mobilisation preparation began in earnest. More funds were made available for the army, which had fallen behind the other two services in level of preparedness, and a great effort was made to provide a large and modern air defence system based around radar and the most advanced monoplane fighters. By 1939, though no earlier, Britain was more prepared for a large war than her critics or enemies supposed (**99, 109**).

How did this arms race affect the diplomatic situation? The mere existence of armaments does not of itself cause war. Rearmament clearly demonstrated the willingness of all the major powers involved to consider war as a future possible course of action, but until 1939 none of the powers, Germany included, was in a position militarily to risk major war. Rearmament plans took much time to complete. German plans were geared towards a major war in the mid-1940s. Detailed military campaign planning had only just

Table 1 Military expenditure in Britain, France and Germany, 1932–39

	France		Britain		Germany	
	A	B	A	B	A	B
	(billion fr.)	(%)	(£ million)	(%)	(billion RM.)	(%)
1932	13.8	5.0	103.3	2.5	0.76	0.8
1933	13.4	5.2	107.6	3.0	1.2	1.9
1934	11.6	4.9	113.9	3.0	3.6	4.1
1935	12.8	5.8	137.0	2.0	5.4	6.0
1936	15.1	6.3	185.9	5.0	10.2	10.8
1937	21.5	7.1	256.3	7.0	10.9	11.7
1938	29.1	8.6	397.4	8.0	17.2	17.2
1939	93.6	23.0	719.0	22.0	38.0	30.0

A Total expenditure at current prices
B Expenditure as a percentage of national income

Figures for financial year 1 April – 31 March

Sources: France (**60**, pp. 35, 303): Britain (**109**, p. 297): Germany, in Overy, R. J. 'The German Motorisierung and Rearmament' *Economic History Review* 2nd Ser., vol 32, 1979, p. 113.

Table 2 Aircraft production in Britain, France and Germany*, 1933–40

	Britain	France	Germany
1933	633	n.a.	368
1934	740	n.a.	1,968
1935	1,140	785	3,183
1936	1,877	890	5,112
1937	2,153	743	5,606
1938	2,827	1,382	5,235
1939	7,940	3,163	8,295
1940	15,049	2,113	10,247

* includes combat and non-combat aircraft

Source: Overy, R. J. *The Air War 1939–1945*, Europa, 1980, pp. 21, 150.

begun in Germany in 1939. British and French preparations, on the other hand, were planned to peak in 1939–40, since they could not afford a sustained high level of rearmament without risking political and economic crisis. Chamberlain would have preferred this increase in military force to act primarily as a deterrent against further aggression, but there can be no doubt that British and French policy in 1939 was powerfully influenced by the mounting evidence that the west was temporarily in a position not simply to deter, were that possible, but also to fight. This involved a great risk for both powers. Indeed there have been many critics then and since, who argued that Britain and France should have armed far sooner and to a much greater extent, since this might have avoided the element of risk altogether. But this is to ignore the many pressures on both governments – and for that matter on Hitler too – which made a faster rate of rearmament difficult to achieve however pressing its necessity.

Finance, industry and labour

The scale and speed of rearmament depended on the extent to which Britain, Germany and France could cope with the constraints placed on their military preparations through finance, industrial capacity and shortages of labour. These were the major determinants of the economic effort behind rearmament. They assumed a special significance because the military planners in all three countries expected a future war to be won by the degree of economic mobilisation each could achieve.

Preparation for total war was very expensive. To find the necessary sums in peace-time invited a whole range of difficulties: a reduction in living standards, the prospect of inflation, excessive government borrowing (excessive, that is, by the orthodox financial standards of the 1930s) and cut-backs in social programmes. These risks seemed all the greater in a Europe slowly recovering from the effects of the world recession. Governments were reluctant to risk fragile financial stability for the sake of large-scale armaments. In Germany this produced a growing crisis by 1936. Rearmament of limited scope had contributed to the rapid recovery of the German economy. In 1936 Hitler wanted to use this stronger economy to accelerate rearmament well beyond the levels originally planned. Schacht and the orthodox bankers and industrialists objected that Germany could not afford the cost, and should concentrate instead on exports. Germany had experienced the damaging hyper-inflation of 1923. Large expenditure on arms carried the risk of inflation once again, and with it the possibility of political unrest. Hitler's answer was to bring the economy more closely under state control and party influence. The financial markets in Germany were strictly regulated. Government loans were floated to pay for rearmament and taxes were raised. Significant cuts were made in the civilian sector from 1938 onwards. The Minister of Finance, Count Schwerin von Krosigk, complained that the sums required to pay for rearmament would, by 1939, cripple the German economy. But in practice the close controls erected over the German economy, backed by the full and brutal authority of the Nazi state, made it possible to increase military expenditure without serious economic crisis.

This prospect seemed far from certain in the western democracies. Fear of the damaging economic and political effects of big increases in government expenditure slowed down the pace of rearmament in both France and Britain. In 1936 and 1937 the Popular Front government in France placed a high priority on social welfare programmes and increased living standards, but also wanted to increase rearmament to meet the Fascist threat. The effect was to undermine orthodox business confidence, accelerate the flight of capital and gold, and weaken the franc. The inflationary impact on the currency undermined efforts to improve living standards and invited a crisis with labour as well. Though new sums for rearmament were raised they required an increase in government debt which threatened budgetary stability. When military expenditure was raised again in the spring of 1938 to even higher levels, Georges Bonnet, the Foreign Minister, painted an alarming picture of the consequences: 'if France should have to continue to arm at the present rate it would be necessary to regiment the entire population, placing the civilian population on soldiers' wages and soldiers' rations' (**39**, p. 27).

British politicians shared this fear of excessive financial burdens. Rearmament was tolerable, Inskip thought, only 'without making demands on our resources which would impair stability'. Chamberlain was haunted 'with the sense that the burden of armaments might break our backs' (**91**). Britain, too, was concerned to maintain political and economic stability by not sacrificing too readily either living standards or social expenditure. Nevertheless the pressure of international events after 1936 pushed the government towards increased military outlays. Recent research has shown that the conventional view of the Treasury and Bank of England resisting the financial demands of rearmament must be modified (**99**). The Treasury ensured that the money was spent as effectively as possible, and would release no funds without a good case for their necessity, but in the end no serious constraints were placed on rearmament by a shortage of finance. Rearmament was met by a combination of tax increases, government loans and budget deficits, £15 million in 1937–38, £137 million in 1938–39. Only when the very great increases in arms spending were proposed in 1938 (£1,650 million over five years) did the situation worsen. The Chancellor of the Exchequer, Sir John Simon, opposed the increases on the grounds that 'it is impossible to escape the conclusion that we were advancing to a position in which the financial situation would get altogether out of hand' (**109**, p. 237). When the figure was raised to £2,000 million Simon warned the cabinet, in the same way as his German counterpart had done, of impending economic collapse. But by then Britain was too firmly committed to war preparation. Despite their fears for the worst, Treasury officials provided the funds that the services wanted as they did in France and Germany.

Finance as such was not the main constraint on the arms race. The main problem was one of resources: factory capacity, raw materials and labour. Finance only became a serious problem when the shortage of resources involved the purchase of goods from abroad, since this put great pressure on the balance of payments and on supplies of foreign exchange and gold. The critical factor here was raw materials. All three powers were short of basic strategic materials. Britain and Germany had adequate coal supplies, but limited amounts of iron ore. France had inadequate supplies of coal, more iron ore, some bauxite for aluminium, but little else. France imported 100 per cent of its rubber, 99 per cent of its oil, 100 per cent of its copper, nickel and manganese (**147**). To increase arms output all three powers were forced to import materials from abroad. This raised the problem of how to pay for the extra imports. Some of them were paid for by liquidating investments held abroad, but this was a temporary solution. Germany used up these sources in 1936 and 1937, but Britain and France were both reluctant to prejudice their declining investment position abroad by liquidating their assets, since these investments were supposed to be a source of strength in time of war. Nor did they wish to frighten financial and trading circles too much by introducing greater government control of foreign trade. The other alternative was to pay for imports by increased exports. But the problem here was that rearmament (for which imports were necessary) reduced the amount of industrial capacity available for the export industries, and produced instead a balance of payments crisis.

There were a number of ways round this dilemma. In Germany Hitler ordered the development of a vast programme of substitute production, using domestic resources to avoid having to pay for imports. In addition stringent controls were set up over gold and currency transactions to make sure that Germany could pay for what she needed abroad. Exports were subsidised and special trading agreements set up which gave Germany privileged access to raw materials. The incorporation of Austria and the occupation of Czechoslovakia brought additional gold and foreign exchange resources into the Reich.

These were all solutions not open to the western powers, with their commitment to liberal economics and the free market, and under strong pressure from the United States after the Exchange Equalisation Agreement of 1936 not to interfere with the exchange system. In France the situation was especially serious in 1936 and 1937. The flight of gold, caused by loss of confidence at home, weakened the franc and forced a series of devaluations that left the franc at a third of its 1929 value by 1938. This meant dearer imports, which made rearmament still more expensive. Nor could France benefit from increased exports, which a cheaper franc might have encouraged, because of the relative inefficiency of much of French industry and increased labour costs with the coming of the forty-hour week (**76**). Britain's hope of expanding exports from the staple industries to pay for imports broke down because of the general crisis in world trade. The domestic recovery in Britain was fuelled by home demand rather than exports, the exact opposite of what was required to cope with rearmament. Yet the expansion of the arms sector threatened to reduce home demand and divert foreign trade away from civilian goods, which was electorally unpopular. Nor could the government easily compel industry and commerce to adopt strategic and military priorities, because of the strong political resistance to interference with the market. In the end the British government opted to run ever larger balance of payments deficits – £55 million in 1937–38, £70 million in 1939 – and accept all the risks that this involved in weakening Britain's economic position abroad.

The result, while not critical before 1939, was highly undesirable. Both France and Britain experienced a severe fall in gold reserves, the former in 1936–38, the latter in 1938–39. British holdings of gold fell from over £800 million in the spring of 1938 to £460 million by the outbreak of war. This was caused partly by having to pay for extra imports for rearmament, but it also reflected declining confidence by foreign investors. The lack of confidence then spread to the pound which experienced what was then considered to be a considerable drop in value against the dollar, falling from a high of $5 in February 1938 to $4.66 a year later (**136**). This involuntary devaluation increased pressure on the balance of payments even more, since it made imports more expensive, and came at a time when rearmament was diverting all available resources away from exporting. British and French efforts to increase the resources available for war by buying large quantities of material and equipment from the United States only made things worse. Exchange controls might at this stage have eased the difficulties, but would have invited retaliation from the United States and have slowed down the pace of rearmament. Instead Britain was forced to make the first concessions to the United States on British protection in the form of a trade agreement signed in November 1938. The western powers were caught in a vicious circle. Unable now to cut back on rearmament from fear of Germany, Italy and Japan, the western powers were creating a situation which called in question their ability to sustain a war of any length or to preserve domestic economic stability [**doc. 12**]. 'We are sailing', reflected a Treasury official, 'upon uncharted waters to an unknown destination' (**109**, p. 276).

Labour was also a critical factor in rearmament. There was no shortage of labour of a general kind. But rearmament required large numbers of skilled workers in engineering, metal-working and construction. Much of the unemployed workforce available in both Britain and France was located in staple industries, away from the main areas of arms production and lacking the skills needed by the arms industry. Skilled workers were the most likely to find employment once the economic recovery began and by 1936 were already working in a range of non-war industries. The difficulty lay in diverting these employed resources away from civilian or export production into arms work. In Germany the situation became serious as early as 1936. Under the Four-Year Plan stringent labour controls were introduced which involved direction of skilled labour into war work and schemes for retraining and apprenticeship. But in practice the controls were difficult to enforce. German firms remained short of skilled labour up to the outbreak of war and beyond, a fact that held back the efforts to convert greater capacity to war work.

In Britain and France labour controls, though discussed, were rejected as unworkable. Efforts were made to increase training schemes, and higher wages were used to attract labour from civilian into military industry. But this brought with it certain dangers. The removal of skilled workers from a firm might have the effect of making the less skilled workforce redundant, thereby increasing the level of unemployment, already very high. The 1938 slump did some of the work for the government by releasing civilian labour at a critical point in the rearmament effort, but not enough. Both governments favoured greater use of machinery and capital equipment which could be operated by semi-skilled or unskilled labour. Since rearmament required the large-scale production of standard weapons and components this made considerable sense. But it produced widespread resistance from the skilled workforce, who feared the effects on job security and wage levels of the dilution of skilled labour. In Britain the engineering workers, with recent memories of the depression, were particularly sensitive to this threat. Efforts to dilute and de-skill were therefore resisted. The unions not only feared the loss of skills but also distrusted the whole rearmament programme, which they saw as a temporary boom before the onset of a further period of recession and unemployment (**135**). Only the worsening international situation, and the promise of job guarantees after the emergency, persuaded labour to co-operate with the scheme. Labour relations in French factories were if anything more strained, soured by two or three years of lock-outs, strikes, factory occupations and wage restraint. Faced with a hostile workforce and international insecurity, French businessmen were slow to re-equip until large sums for investment were provided by the state in 1939. The Daladier government used indirect methods to push more labour towards the war industries, cutting home demand and state civilian expenditure to do so, and reversing the trend to shorter working hours initiated by the Popular Front.

Rearmament and domestic politics

The hostility of labour raised an important issue for all three powers. To what extent would large-scale rearmament jeopardise domestic political stability? All the states involved in the arms race were forced to face this question. Domestic political stability was equated with a stable economy and the maintenance of living standards. War preparation threatened economic stability and, it was feared, would lead to a sharpening of political conflict between left and right.

There is no doubt that British rearmament, certainly in its early stages, was affected by this fear. The Conservative Party, the dominant partner in the National Government, had to balance the problems of the international system against the prospect of political survival at home. Baldwin and Chamberlain had committed the party in 1935 to a programme of social expenditure and house building which they were reluctant to abandon for a rearmament programme whose full urgency was not yet apparent either to the government or the public. Labour's attitude to even this limited rearmament provoked Chamberlain to write that: 'All the elements of danger are here . . . I can see that we might easily run, in no time, into a series of crippling strikes and finally the defeat of the Government and the advent of an ignorant, unprepared and heavily pledged opposition' (**58**, p. 292). Though the situation never became as serious as Conservatives believed it might, their foreign policy was governed to a considerable extent by fear both of alienating labour and of the price that might have to be paid (wage increases, union recognition, greater support for the League and so on) to win labour co-operation. Above all was the fear of creating another economic crisis as severe as 1929–31 before the general election due in 1940. This political balancing act also had to be performed with industry. Though there was no question of businessmen preferring Labour to Conservative, there was a danger that rearmament would provoke resistance to excessive state control, government spending and labour policies. In 1935 business leaders warned Chamberlain that they would only co-operate with large-scale rearmament on their own terms. All of this put pressure on the government to tread warily with rearmament, and to seek for as long as possible a settlement of outstanding international issues.

In France the link between politics and defence spending was clear. High military expenditure had contributed to the fall of the Blum government. The right-wing Daladier government that followed the Popular Front was just as alarmed by the prospect that further increases in rearmament expenditure would lead to a decline in living standards and to popular unrest. From 1938 onwards Daladier ruled through decree laws, by-passing parliamentary opposition. In November 1938 a General Strike was called in Paris to protest against wage cuts and increased hours, though it was defeated by firm government action [**doc. 13**]. The government remained very alive to the threat of widespread popular unrest. Even before the outbreak of war, using as an excuse the pact made between Germany and Russia, it moved to outlaw the French Communist Party in order to weaken domestic resistance to new labour legislation and mobilisation plans (**39**).

Germany, despite the fact that it had an authoritarian government, was not immune from considerations of this kind. During 1936 and 1937 a political struggle was fought out between the Nazi Party, the military and German business over the future direction of the economy. The groups led by Schacht sought greater accommodation with the west and a return to freer trade and lower levels of arms spending. They feared that otherwise the economy would collapse beneath the strain and thereby revive the threat of Communism which had so frightened German conservatives during the depression. Nazi leaders wanted the opposite: higher levels of armaments, greater autarky and an independent foreign policy. It was this view that prevailed. Schacht was forced to resign in November 1937, and in 1938 Hitler purged the armed forces and the cabinet of opponents of his strategy. Popular resistance was necessarily more muted, reaching a high point in the summer of 1936. It was suppressed partly by sheer brutality and terror, partly by Hitler's insistence on controlling prices and wages and raising taxes on higher incomes in an effort to spread economic sacrifices more evenly. By 1939, when rearmament reached a level three times greater than in 1936, the apparatus of repression was much more developed. The shortages of goods and low wage levels provoked no serious political response, though the Nazi state always remained sensitive to its possibility (**98**).

It was in the western powers that the problems of rearmament, finance and domestic politics were most acute. Fears of financial crisis and political unrest held Britain and France back from a substantial effort of rearmament until 1938, and encouraged both governments to explore the possibility of a settlement rather than run the risks of collapse at home. It can now be seen that the political risks were much exaggerated. Labour in both countries was strongly anti-Fascist, and quite unprepared to bring governments down on the grounds of excessive military spending. If anything, sections of the left became increasingly critical of the governments for not taking firmer action at an earlier date. But nevertheless the fact remained that governments perceived rearmament as a political problem. As such it had to be weighed in the scales when reaching decisions about the size and timing of the rearmament effort. By 1938–39 economic crisis appeared a very real possibility and the political dangers greater than ever. The high levels of arms spending could be sustained for only a short time, while the last unemployed resources were used up and before the balance of payments became critical. This fact pushed both governments towards the conclusion that it would be better to take decisive action, even war, sooner rather than later. German preparations pointed to a war in the mid-1940s. For Britain and France the decisive year was 1939.

5   War over Poland

The aftermath of Munich

In the immediate afterglow of Munich it seemed at last that
Europe was close to the general settlement Chamberlain wanted.
His ambition in November 1938 was 'to arrive at a stabilisation
of Europe' (**101**, p. 152). There was a general sense of *détente*, and
great relief at home that war had been averted. Britain and
Germany signed the Anglo-German agreement, followed a few
weeks later by the ratification in Rome of an Anglo-Italian understanding reached the previous April. French and German negotiators in December signed a further agreement expressing mutual
goodwill and respect of frontiers [**doc. 14**]. In January Chamberlain and his Foreign Secretary, Lord Halifax, visited Mussolini to
try to reach a settlement of the Mediterranean area as a prelude
to a more comprehensive agreement with Hitler on colonies and
economic co-operation, which the British foreign office had been
working on since early 1938. There even appeared the danger,
though a remote one, that Britain and France might each try to
reach a separate agreement with the dictators to safeguard their
own interests, a fear that prompted the British to agree at last to
full military discussions between British and French general staffs.

Yet at the same time could be detected a very different mood
in British and French governing circles. There had always been,
as we have seen, implicit limits to appeasement. It was now felt that
the time had come to state clearly what they were. Though there
was by no means unanimity on what exactly constituted these
limits, there was general agreement that in 1939 they were likely
to be put to the test. Evidence from both Germany and Italy,
supplied in part by the German 'moderates' themselves, suggested
that the dictators might carry out what the British Foreign Office
called a 'mad-dog act' in the near future. It was foolhardy under
these circumstances for the western powers to place much confidence in *détente*. Instead Chamberlain insisted that the pace of rearmament should not be allowed to slacken: 'it was clear that it
would be madness for the country to stop rearming until we were

convinced that other countries would act in the same way . . . we should relax no particle of effort' (**109**, p. 233).

Both governments, however, agreed that there was not much point in contesting Germany's position in central Europe. Hitler, Halifax thought, should be allowed to 'go ahead and do what he liked' there, but he should not be allowed to trespass any further [**doc. 15**]. Switzerland, Holland and Belgium were deemed to be areas of vital interest in the west. In eastern Europe it was agreed that Britain and France should try to hold the line Poland-Romania-Yugoslavia. Danzig was not yet considered an essential interest. To this list was added the 'vital cord' of western communications through the Mediterranean, and with it the defence of Tunisia, Egypt, Greece and Turkey. To this end the British and French began to explore between January and March 1939 the prospect of an eastern Locarno, a collective guarantee, if possible including the Soviet Union, of the remaining frontiers of eastern Europe (**91, 101**).

German reaction to the Munich agreement was quite different. Though Hitler was willing to sign expressions of goodwill with Britain and France he assumed that he had been given at Munich a green light in the east. This was an understandable miscalculation. German power was now a fact of life in eastern Europe. Britain and France had demonstrated in September how unwilling they were to risk war to contest this fact. A new arrogance entered into Germany's relations with her eastern neighbours. On 21 October 1938, less than a month after signing the Munich Pact, Hitler ordered his generals to prepare for the elimination of the Czech state and the return of Memel to the Reich. The first stage of German imperialism, *Mitteleuropa*, now seemed within Hitler's grasp without a major war. Germany rejected Chamberlain's offer of discussions on colonies and economic agreements. Instead Germany tied the economies of eastern Europe more closely to her own. The rump state of Czechoslovakia was treated like a colony, compelled through its weakness to reach unfavourable economic agreements with Germany. The integrity of the Czech state was undermined by deliberate German efforts to encourage Slovak separatism. On 15 March 1939 the Czech president was forced to invite German troops to enter Czechoslovakia on the pretext that it was now ungovernable and faced with incipient civil war. The Third Reich occupied Bohemia and Moravia under a protectorate,

Opposite: *Germany and central Europe 1933–9*

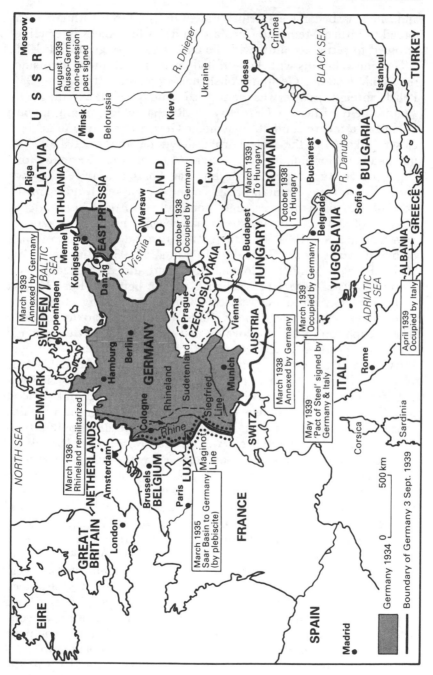

The following text labels appear on the map:

Moscow

August 1939
Russo-German
non-agression
pact signed

U S S R

R. Dnieper

Crimea

BLACK SEA

TURKEY

Istanbul

Odessa

Ukraine

Kiev

Minsk

Belorussia

LATVIA

Riga

LITHUANIA

Memel

March 1939
Annexed by Germany

BALTIC
SEA

EAST PRUSSIA

Königsberg

Danzig

Warsaw

P O L A N D

R. Vistula

October 1938
Occupied by Germany

Lvov

March 1939
To Hungary

ROMANIA

Bucharest

R. Danube

BULGARIA

Sofia

GREECE

ALBANIA

April 1939
Occupied by Italy

ADRIATIC
SEA

YUGOSLAVIA

Belgrade

March 1939
Occupied by Germany

Budapest

HUNGARY

October 1938
To Hungary

Vienna

AUSTRIA

CZECHOSLOVAKIA

Prague

Sudetenland

March 1938
Annexed by Germany

Munich

Siegfried
Line

SWITZ.

ITALY

Rome

Corsica

Sardinia

May 1939
'Pact of Steel' signed by
Germany & Italy

SWEDEN

Copenhagen

DENMARK

Hamburg

Berlin

GERMANY

Cologne

Rhineland

Rhine

March 1936
Rhineland remilitarized

NETHERLANDS

Amsterdam

NORTH SEA

Brussels

BELGIUM

LUX.

Maginot
Line

March 1935
Saar Basin to Germany
(by plebiscite)

Paris

FRANCE

GREAT
BRITAIN

London

EIRE

SPAIN

Madrid

500 km

Germany 1934   0

Boundary of Germany 3 Sept. 1939

61

and Slovakia became a satellite state. On 21 March Lithuania was forced to return Memel to German hands. A few weeks later Hitler resolved to settle accounts with Poland at some stage during 1939.

German relations with Poland had been distant but cordial since the signing of the German-Polish non-aggression treaty in 1934. Polish foreign policy was concerned chiefly with avoiding any commitment either to Germany or Russia which might involve Poland in a future conflict. Spasmodic German attempts to achieve closer links with the Poles broke down on this doctrine of an independent foreign policy. After Munich the German tone changed. It was hoped in Berlin that Poland would be drawn naturally into the German orbit. Poland was asked to give up the port of Danzig which, though nominally a Free City under a League of Nations commission, had been run by a Nazi city government since 1934. In return Poland would receive guarantees of her integrity from Germany. In January 1939 Hitler met the Polish Foreign Minister, Colonel Beck, and added the demand for German access across the Polish Corridor between East Prussia and the Reich. The Poles refused to consider the suggestions. The demand for Danzig, said Beck, 'must inevitably lead to conflict'. The occupation of Czechoslovakia and the cession of Memel made the Polish position much weaker; German demands became more insistent and uncompromising. In secret Hitler revealed his true plans for Poland: 'It is not Danzig that is at stake. For us it is a matter of expanding our living space in the east and making food supplies secure . . .' Polish economic and labour resources, like those of Czechoslovakia and Austria, were needed to build up German strength for the great war in the future [**doc. 16**]. Hitler was confident that this could be achieved without a general war. His anglophobe Foreign Minister, Ribbentrop, argued that Britain and France were weak, declining powers, who would seek any solution, however shoddy, to avoid having to fight. This belief played a vital part in Hitler's decision to compel Poland, by force if necessary, to come within the German sphere.

This, in the end, was to be a costly miscalculation. The German occupation of Prague was confirmation, if confirmation were needed, that Hitler could not be restrained by paper guarantees. It forced both the French and British governments to give firm expression to their strategy of containing the dictator powers, which had been slowly taking shape since Munich. It would be wrong to see Prague as the point at which enfeebled appeasers were finally compelled by an outraged public to stand up to the dictators. Both before and after Prague, western strategy was guided by the desire to reach a European settlement on British and French terms, backed up by rising military power to be used only at the point where vital British and French interests were at stake. It was not until the spring of 1939 that the limits of this policy were finally reached. Rightly or wrongly, Britain and France now saw the problem in terms of their survival as great powers, with all the prestige, political influence and economic advantage that this status bestowed.

In the weeks after Prague the British and French searched for some way of making this situation clear to Hitler. Since they had been exploring the possibility of guarantees in eastern Europe for some months, it was decided that a firm gesture should now be made in that direction, particularly as there now existed the possibility that Poland might be pushed into the arms of Germany if the west held back. Chamberlain argued for a four-power declaration, including Russia, to guarantee Polish independence. Poland was unhappy with any agreement that left her dependent on Russian goodwill, and Stalin anyway rejected what he saw as western efforts to get Russia, in his words, 'to pull the chestnuts out of the fire'. What Poland wanted was a bilateral pact with Britain. After some hesitation the British government accepted, worried that without an immediate gesture the whole Balkan region might fall under German domination. On 31 March Britain gave an open guarantee to Poland [**doc. 17**] to intervene in the event of any threat to her independence, though it carried the rider that the Poles 'would not indulge in provocative behaviour or stupid obstinacy either generally or in particular as regards Danzig' (**91**, p. 202).

The British saw the Polish guarantee as a prelude to a more general set of alliances. From a policy of no formal commitment Britain embarked on a scrambled search for allies in the Balkans and the Mediterranean. Romania was regarded as a key power, and when the French government, delighted to have got an eastern European commitment from Britain for the first time, asked for a guarantee of Romanian frontiers too, the British agreed. Neither Romania nor Yugoslavia would be drawn into any effort to encircle Germany, however, and instead moved closer to the Axis powers. The only real successes for British diplomacy were closer ties with Greece and Turkey, which were both alarmed at the sudden change in the balance of power in the Balkans following the occupation of Czechoslovakia.

Analysis

Mussolini had been as disturbed by the German *coup* in Prague as the western powers. His initial reaction was one of hurt pride that his fellow dictator could leave him as ignorant of his intentions as everyone else. There was even talk of moving closer to Britain and France. Instead Mussolini, backed up by Fascist Party leaders, decided to embark on his own foreign policy initiatives to show Hitler that he, too, was capable of taking on the inert power of Britain and France. On 30 March he ordered the occupation of Albania, which had been for some time an Italian satellite in all but name, and announced that the Balkans and eastern Mediterranean should now be regarded as the Italian sphere of influence. Hitler was content to see Mussolini turn southwards, since it would occupy the British and French while he settled the Polish question. Somewhat to his surprise Mussolini then proposed a close military alliance between the two powers which was signed on 22 May in Berlin. The 'Pact of Steel', as it was called, required each power to help the other unconditionally in the event of war. Mussolini justified this commitment on the grounds that it gave a formal and equal partnership in place of the growing inferiority that had characterised Italian relations with Germany since the *Anschluss* (**85**).

The Pact of Steel upset British and French calculations that Mussolini might be detached from Germany as part of the strategy of containing Hitler. It confirmed popular French mistrust and hostility towards Italy and led to a strengthening of military ties between the two western powers. France was at last successful in her efforts to get the British government to introduce conscription and to provide a firm commitment to intervene militarily on the continent. During the summer months British and French general staffs discussed the allocation of tasks. Poland, with its army of fifty-four divisions, was reckoned to be a useful addition to the Allies' armoury. By the time Britain gave a further, unequivocal guarantee to Poland on 25 August, preparations for armed conflict with the Axis powers in the immediate future were well advanced (**46, 73**).

Why did Britain and France choose to risk a major war in the summer of 1939? A popular answer is that war was thrust upon them by the insatiable appetite of the Axis powers, which public opinion in Britain and France was no longer prepared to tolerate. Against their will the appeasers were forced to accept the widespread revulsion against Fascism and to stand at the head of a crusade against the totalitarian powers. It is certainly true that political differences at home were suppressed by a rising tide of national sentiment that made it much easier for both governments to make clear after March their determination to defend their vital interests by force. There was also much anti-Fascist idealism which could be used to justify a policy of firmness. But the evidence suggests that Britain and France were determined to take some sort of action and had been building up towards that point since the spring of 1938 when rearmament was set fully in motion. At least some of the change in public opinion was engineered by the government and not the other way around. Both populations had to be persuaded over the summer that Danzig was a cause worth fighting for where the Sudetenland was not. Of course Danzig was not the cause of the conflict for the Allies either, but was the instrument whereby public opinion could be shown the intransigent and evil nature of German ambitions. This gave a moral gloss to what was in fact a decision about when was the best time to fight for Britain and France, not for Poland.

If this seems a harsh judgement, it is a realistic one. If Britain and France had not put themselves in a position in which they felt able to run the risk of declaring war on their terms, then Poland might well have been sacrificed as had Czechoslovakia, public opinion or not. There were prominent politicians on both sides of the Channel who thought this the most reasonable course right up to September 1939. But in fact the British and French decision for war in 1939 was based on what they perceived as a temporarily more favourable set of international and domestic circumstances, reinforced by the economic and military necessity of waging war as soon as possible. The alternative to not fighting, if Germany refused to back down, was to sacrifice this opportunity and to forfeit their status as first-class powers. 'France', observed Daladier in November 1938, had to choose 'between a slow decline or a renaissance through effort' (**89**, p. 247).

During the course of 1939 a number of new elements of particular value to the Allies were brought into the crisis. The British Dominions, which had favoured appeasement up to and beyond the Munich crisis, now moved towards giving positive support to the Allies in the event of a European conflict. More important still the United States, although formally committed both to neutrality and to the ideal of collective efforts for peace and disarmament, drew informally closer to the western powers. Chamberlain found Roosevelt 'wary but helpful'. While keeping the isolationists at bay, Roosevelt tried to find ways of supplying Britain and France with arms and materials without abandoning neutrality. The cash-and-carry principle incorporated in the Neutrality Act allowed the western powers to collect non-war materials without undue difficulty. The long lists of aviation equipment which the French and British drew up after Munich were a different matter. Only the insistence of the American air forces that this was a convenient way to get someone else to pay for the early stages of America's own rearmament persuaded the President to accept the orders, although to do so meant a confrontation with Congress (**65**). What was more important to the Allies was the fact that America, whether she liked it or not, was assuming more of the responsibility in the Far East for keeping Japan in check. Japanese foreign policy was constricted by the long-drawn-out Chinese war and by fear of Russia, with whom Japan found herself in armed conflict during 1939 along the Manchurian-Siberian border. Hitler's attempt to get the Japanese to sign a formal military alliance early in 1939 was rejected in Tokyo for fear of alienating the other major Pacific powers while Japan was still fighting the war in China.

The United States would not, on the other hand, give any kind of formal commitment to the Allies. This for Chamberlain was the ideal solution. As long as America confined herself to supplying economic resources, Britain and France would not be too dependent on the United States when it came to confronting Hitler. If Britain and France waited longer, then economic dependence would be much greater, and America might well set political conditions, such as colonial self-government and an end to protection, as a price for further help. This would make explicit the decline of Britain and France as great powers and produce the same long-term effect as the failure to confront Germany. These were devious, even wrong-headed, calculations; so devious that some Americans believed that the British and French were secretly planning to build an anti-American economic bloc in Europe with Hitler's co-operation, a solution that had certainly been voiced in official circles, though never seriously considered. In their turn the British, with some justice, harboured the suspicion that if the United States became more involved in Europe's affairs, the effect on the Empire would be very damaging. It was perceived to be more in the Allies' interests to keep America at a distance as a friendly, rich neutral while they faced up to Germany themselves (**89, 103**).

The second factor that weighed heavily in the scales in 1939 was the relative shift in the military balance in Europe. By the autumn of 1939 both Britain and France were much stronger than they had been at the time of Munich. As they intended, the great rearmament programmes were now bearing fruit. British rearmament was geared to reach a peak in 1939–40. The air plans laid down in 1935 had aimed at this date; so too did the four-year plan laid down in the Defence White Paper in 1936. The air defence programme based around radar and modern fighter aircraft was near completion in the summer of 1939. When Chamberlain asked the head of the Supply Board in July 1938 when he could expect armaments roughly on equal terms with Germany he replied 'in a year' (**58**, p. 35). Hankey, chairman of the Defence Requirements Committee, gave Chamberlain the same date, mid-1939, when Britain could begin to feel secure militarily.

French rearmament was at last in full swing too. British and French tank and aircraft production was greater than that of Germany by 1939 and, of more importance, was known to be so through military intelligence. Although there was still widespread public alarm at Allied unpreparedness, there was growing confidence in the government that Allied strength was now more evenly weighted against that of Germany. These were compelling arguments. Chamberlain hoped that the Allies' forces were sufficiently strong to deter Germany altogether from risking an armed confrontation. But whether the western powers fought or only deterred Hitler, the favourable military balance could not be expected to last. To a greater extent than Germany, the western powers were trapped in a military timetable of their own choosing. This created the necessity of opposing Hitler at what they saw as the best moment.

This growing confidence was augmented by a stream of intelligence information from Germany and Italy which suggested that both powers faced growing economic crises and would not be able to risk, let alone sustain, a major conflict. The British military attaché in Berlin supplied evidence that Germany would not be ready for a major war for a number of years, since she did not yet have sufficient control over the newly won resources of central and eastern Europe [**doc. 18**]. These reports confirmed the assessment by the Economic Intelligence department that the German economy was now stretched taut and might collapse with the first push. This view fitted well with the Allied strategy of blockade and economic warfare. The prospects for actually defeating Germany were better than they had been since the mid-1930s, but could not be expected to last. It was thought that German strength would

increase, once it was magnified by the use of eastern European resources that would save Germany from the effects of blockade, while
that of the Allies would relatively decline. By 1942, it was argued,
the situation might have deteriorated so far as to make a declaration
of war impossible.

Nor were the Allies immune from the prospect of economic
crisis. Though they were certain that their current financial and
commercial strength was greater than Germany's, a high level of
readiness for war could not be sustained without the real prospect
of economic and political difficulties at home. The Chancellor of
the Exchequer urged this view throughout the summer. Oliver
Stanley, the President of the Board of Trade, drew the conclusion
that 'there would come a moment which, on a balance of our
financial strength and our strength in armaments, was the best
time for war to break out' (**109**, p. 280). The danger of inflation
fuelled by a high level of government borrowing was expected to
develop from the autumn of 1939 onwards as unemployed
resources were gradually used up. The run on gold and foreign
exchange reserves could not be sustained indefinitely without stringent controls which might well prejudice important parts of the
arms programme, and would almost certainly have made it difficult to get further American co-operation. If the 'fourth arm of
defence' were to weigh in the scales at all, then it was clear that
it would be better for the Allies to use the threat of war, or war
itself, in 1939 or in 1940 at the latest (**137**).

All of these were pressing arguments for confronting Hitler. Of
course they did not make war inevitable. If Hitler had not put
pressure on Poland, war would not have been necessary at all, at
least not in September 1939. Nor would war have been the
outcome if Hitler had agreed to accept the conditions laid down
by the Allies for a settlement. There were many opportunities
extended to Germany to adopt a position acceptable to Britain and
France, broadly those laid down at Munich. But in 1939 the Allies
made it clear that any settlement had to be within those terms,
which to the Germans was tantamount to an admission that they
enjoyed their great-power status only at the behest of Britain and
France. This was the solution that the Allies would have preferred:
to use their armed might to force Hitler to back down without the
horrors of another great war. No one, least of all Chamberlain,
wanted such a war; but he accepted the possibility of war with
gloomy dignity, torn between his conviction that in an ideal world
compromise was always possible and his reluctant acceptance that

in practice it was not. Right up to the last, every effort was made
to get Hitler to see the reality of his situation and the futility of
war.

The Russian factor

Diplomatic reality meant something very different to Hitler than
it did to Chamberlain. He had predicted in November 1937 that
Britain and France would make no serious effort to save eastern
Europe. Events had borne out this conclusion. By March 1939 he
had achieved almost all that he wanted for the first stage of
German expansion. It seemed both unlikely and unreasonable to
expect the western powers to fight for Poland when they had for-
gone everything else. 'Our task', he explained in May 1939, 'is to
isolate Poland. There must be no simultaneous conflict with the
western powers' (**98**, p. 90). To make sure of this outcome,
German leaders actively sought to create a set of diplomatic
circumstances which they felt would almost certainly secure non-
intervention.

The strategy chosen was to neutralise, if possible, either the
Soviet Union or Britain, or both. Ribbentrop and the German
Foreign Office explored the first possibility, while Goering pursued
the second. The British gambit was not played with any urgency
or consistency, since Germany did not want to reach another firm
agreement as she had at Munich, unless the terms amounted to
a free hand in eastern Europe. Rather the object was to persuade
Britain of the reasonableness of the German case and, through
German willingness to talk, to place Britain in a position of uncertainty until she could be faced with a swift coup in Poland which
could not be effectively reversed. In all this Goering played a
calculated role as a man of greater moderation than Hitler, whose
good offices might be used to make Hitler more conciliatory. There
were few on the British side who took Goering's role very seriously,
though it did have the effect, as Hitler and Goering hoped, of
confusing the British government in the weeks before the outbreak
of war as it weighed up the flow of conflicting information
emanating from Berlin (**98**).

For Hitler the Russian strategy was far more important, for it
avoided a repeat of the July Crisis of 1914. If Russia could be
neutralised, then the danger in the west would recede. Otherwise
there existed the threat, made clear by the Franco-British efforts
to construct a four-power agreement with Poland and Russia in

March 1939, of a revival of the pre-war *entente* alliance against Germany. This fear had first become apparent before Munich when it seemed possible that Stalin would intervene in Czechoslovakia if the French would honour their pledge as well. The evidence about Russia's real intentions at the time of Munich is conflicting (**123**). As it was, neither Poland nor Romania would allow the passage of Soviet troops to aid the Czechs, and the French abandoned their commitment, leaving Stalin free to do nothing. In the months after Munich German leaders began to explore the possibility of reaching some sort of agreement with Russia that would remove her as a menace to Germany's domination of eastern Europe. The possibility of just such a move had not escaped the British, who regarded Stalin as a mere opportunist. They, too, began to sound out the prospects of bringing Russia into an eastern alliance system to restrain Hitler.

From a position of diplomatic isolation Stalin found himself, after Munich, courted by both the Axis and western powers. He trusted neither of them. Hitler's Germany was the sworn enemy of Bolshevism. Britain and France were the major imperialist and capitalist powers, capable, Stalin believed, of luring Russia into war to suit their own ends [**doc. 19**]. Russia's chief concern was still to avoid involvement in any major war at all costs. Soviet foreign policy aimed to play one power off against another in the hope of escaping the impending conflict. Stalin offered to the British and French an agreement based on western guarantees for the whole area from the Black Sea to the Baltic. He knew that the west would not be able to accept this, for it was too wide a commitment and involved no reciprocal guarantee from Russia in the west. But it achieved the object of making Germany more interested than ever in neutralising Russia. On 3 May 1939 the Russian foreign minister Litvinov was replaced by Molotov, who was better liked by the Germans. On 30 May the German Foreign Office told their ambassador in Moscow that 'we have now decided to undertake definite negotiations with the Soviet Union' (**113**, p. 272).

The British had reached this decision a few days earlier. There was little enthusiasm for approaches to Russia. 'I must confess the most profound distrust of Russia', said Chamberlain, 'and I distrust her motives, which seem to me to have little connection with our idea of liberty, and to be concerned only with getting every one else by the ears' (**58**, p. 403). Daladier feared that war might hasten Bolshevik domination of the west: 'Cossacks will rule

Europe' (**89**, p. 248). This fear was echoed in the opinion of the British ambassador in Moscow, who thought that Stalin was trying to turn Germany against the west so that the ensuing conflict would weaken the capitalist powers to Russia's advantage. The pursuit of a Russian agreement held other dangers too. It would alienate the eastern European countries that Britain was trying to win over, and it might drive Poland and Spain, both key countries in western calculations, into the arms of Hitler. Nevertheless there were strong pressures in both countries, particularly in France, to establish contacts with Russia. French leaders felt that the Russian factor was vital if Germany were to be restrained from further aggression. The French foreign minister, Georges Bonnet, pinned his faith on the chances of achieving an Anglo-Franco-Soviet pact which would dominate European diplomacy. Halifax and Chamberlain hoped more modestly that Anglo-Russian co-operation could be used to buy support for their foreign policy from the British left and the trade unions, who also supported closer ties with Russia. Even the British chiefs of staff favoured an approach, despite their argument that Russian forces after the purges were for the time being of little military value. They hoped that British discussions with Russia might have the effect of restraining Germany in eastern Europe without having to make any firm commitment to Stalin (**128**).

The failure of the Franco-British efforts to reach agreement with Russia could be traced to the transparent opportunism of western policy, and the failure to co-ordinate the French and British negotiations. Agreement was never pursued with any real enthusiasm, and deep dislike and distrust of Communism coloured western attitudes throughout. It was apparent to the British that Stalin was playing the same game as they were, prolonging negotiation for the effect it would have on Germany. What the British most wanted, Soviet support for Poland in the case of German aggression, could not be pursued too far because of the strong resistance of the Poles to any Russian help. Nor was Stalin prepared to guarantee Poland in this way because it might well leave Russia to bear the brunt of any German attack while the west looked on. Stalin preferred the imperial powers to carry this risk, and was not averse to a shift in the European power balance away from Britain and France, if it strengthened Russia's diplomatic position. In the end the Allies continued discussions, including military talks, throughout the summer in order to alarm the Germans and placate the left. Both had decided (though the French were far less certain) that the

Soviet Union was militarily unprepared and politically unreliable and that Hitler could be challenged without her.

German negotiators were, on the other hand, in a much stronger position. Where the British and French dangled the prospect of war, Hitler offered neutrality, and hints of an eastern settlement favourable to Russia. Realising the value of a Russian agreement to Hitler, Stalin waited until he could be reasonably certain of the British and French intention to fight over Poland before offering anything concrete. As the summer dragged on, Hitler became increasingly worried about whether or not Russia could be detached from the planned Polish conflict. By mid-August the two sides had only reached agreement on economic questions. On 21 August the Germans sent a virtual ultimatum to Moscow asking for a full pact between the two powers. Stalin reacted on his own initiative, and with great haste, in his anxiety to avoid war. Ribbentrop was immediately invited to Moscow and within three days had been offered an agreement in which Germany was compelled to make substantial concessions as she had been a year before at Munich. The Baltic states, Bessarabia and eastern Poland to the River Vistula were assigned as Russian spheres of influence. Both sides agreed to respect each other's frontiers. On 23 August the Nazi-Soviet Non-Aggression Pact was signed [**doc. 20**]. When Hitler heard the news at dinner that night he banged the table and shouted 'I have them'.

Did the Russian factor make any difference to the outbreak of war? It certainly had the effect of convincing Hitler that the western powers could not now intervene to save Poland and that a general war would be averted. On 22 August he told his generals: 'war between Poland and Germany will remain localised . . . England and France will make threats, but will not declare war . . .' (**98**, p. 90). The news of the pact made it seem more certain than in September 1938 that he could run the risk of attacking Poland without general war. To the western powers the pact proved what they had already suspected about Soviet unreliability, but since their strategy was already based on the assumption that Russia would remain isolated from the conflict or would be of little military help even if she joined it, it made much less difference to the decision to go to war than the Germans thought. If anything, the pact meant that Russia would be free to contain Japan in the east, weakening the anti-Comintern powers to the west's advantage. Italy's response was equally favourable to Britain and France. Mussolini was surprised and alarmed by the pact. Within three days of its signature he found a device to withdraw from his hasty obligations in the Pact of Steel, so that he could remain neutral in any conflict over Poland. The Allies no longer had to fear a simultaneous conflict with all three Axis powers. Of course if Britain and France had reached a firm agreement with Russia, Hitler might well have held back from invading Poland and have resorted to diplomatic and economic pressure instead. But this was never a possibility in the circumstances of 1939, particularly since the west had chosen Poland, the most anti-Soviet of the eastern states, as the area where Hitler was to be stopped.

The outbreak of war

The outbreak of a general war in September 1939, though the product of a long period of international crisis and great-power rivalry, had its immediate roots in the illusions and miscalculations about the Polish crisis. Of these the most important was Hitler's belief that the conflict could be isolated; that he could complete his domination of eastern and central Europe, which was for all practical purposes a reality by the beginning of 1939, without general war. From the German point of view in the summer of 1939 there were two possibilities: either that Poland would capitulate without fighting and be drawn into the German camp; or that Poland would be forced to accept German power by a brief military campaign. By August, Hitler had resolved firmly on the latter course. There were moments of hesitation before the Russian Pact was signed, and when Britain and France reiterated their support for Poland on 25 August, and when it became clear that Mussolini was not going to support Germany over Poland after all. However, none of these deflected Hitler from his objective. He convinced himself that his judgement of the west was the right one. Even if the Allies objected to the invasion of Poland, they could not help her militarily and would make mere gestures designed to save face, as they had done in 1938.

The essential flaw in this view was the failure to see that the western powers had reached their limit in 1939. Hitler was right to judge that Poland was not in itself of much intrinsic interest in British and French calculations, but he failed to see that both powers assessed the Polish crisis not on its own merits, but in terms of their global interests and great-power status. To fight for Poland was a means to assert British and French power in the Balkans, the Mediterranean and the Far East as well. Given favourable

Allied intelligence on the military balance, and the threat of severe economic crisis if war preparations were continued at such a high level into the future, the Polish crisis was viewed as an unrepeatable opportunity to challenge German expansion. If war had to come – and the Allies hoped fervently that Hitler would see reason before it did – the late summer of 1939 was a better time to declare it. This was particularly so given the nature of the Allied strategy of blockade and economic warfare, which could be made to bite across the winter months when Hitler would be unable to mount a major land offensive. The only incalculable element was the possibility of German bomb attacks in an effort to achieve the 'knock-out blow' dreamed of by air theorists. Great efforts were made over the summer to complete the necessary civil defence preparations, to arrange the evacuation of women and children, and to prepare for gas attack.

Why did Hitler fail to grasp the Allies' determination in 1939 to contain him? The first reason was the poor intelligence he got on Allied military preparations, which greatly underestimated Allied strength and economic potential. Though Hitler knew that German preparations for major war were far from complete, the evidence he was given by his intelligence sources suggested that British and French rearmament was still far behind. He was fed, too, on a regular diet of ill-informed and highly selective information about the morale and political stability of the democracies [**doc. 21**]. He argued that if he called their bluff over Poland, they would be forced to stand back and would be plunged into political crisis. There was, however, more serious evidence of Allied irresolution. Communications between Poland and the Allies were regularly intercepted, showing that great pressure was being put on the Poles to make reasonable concessions to Berlin over Danzig. All this was resonant of the Czech crisis. The British Ambassador, Nevile Henderson, also gave the impression that the last thing Britain wanted was war, and that it was Polish as much as German intransigence that was the major stumbling block. 'I have held from the beginning', he wrote to London, 'that the Poles were utterly foolish and unwise' (**3**, Vol. 7, p. 198). German discussions with British officials and businessmen during the summer seemed to confirm that in the end Britain might have its price for Poland as it had had for Czechoslovakia [**doc. 22**]. There was thus a good mixture of wishful thinking and justified realism on the German side in their assessment of western intentions.

There was no shortage of illusion in the west either. The stream of information from Berlin, though conflicting, seemed to suggest that Germany was facing severe crisis at home and that the possibility could not be excluded that the German government might be overthrown rather than face war with the west. Chamberlain hoped to the very last that Hitler would be reasonable and would come to terms rather than risk a war he could not win. The prospect of agreement was brought suddenly closer in the last week of August when Goering, apparently on his own initiative but with Hitler's backing, began to talk with the British government through a Swedish intermediary, Birger Dahlerus. The talks showed, however, that even the so-called moderates in Germany were not prepared to accept the major condition for any settlement with Poland, that Germany must show herself willing to work within a political framework acceptable to the western powers; in other words that Germany should reverse her policy of expansion in eastern Europe.

In the middle stood Poland. The Polish government would make no substantial concession to the German position on Danzig or the Polish Corridor [**doc. 23**]. The British and French put pressure on Poland throughout the last weeks of August to make at least some gesture that would conciliate Germany and bring her more readily to the conference table. But the Poles could see that they were faced now with a difficult choice. They could give way to German demands and end up as the Czechs had done, swallowed up piecemeal by the Reich. Or they could remain firm in their defence of Polish sovereignty and independence and face the prospect of fighting Germany. In the end they chose the latter, clinging to the Anglo-French guarantee for want of any alternative, but all too aware of what the likely outcome would be.

These three elements, German illusions, British and French fears for their status as great powers, and Polish firmness, combined together in the last week of August 1939. Hitler postponed the invasion of Poland from 26 August until 31 August on hearing of the renewed British guarantee, and instructed Goering to increase his efforts to detach Britain from France. A flurry of diplomatic activity followed, in which the British sought to buy time by forcing the Poles to send a negotiator to Berlin, as the Germans wanted, so that one last effort could be made to get Hitler to accept British and French terms. Hitler interpreted these efforts as final evidence of the irresolution and timidity of the west. 'Our enemies', he announced, 'have men who are below average. No personalities. No masters, men of action' (**6**). Though there remained an element of risk, as there had been in every move since the occupation of the Rhineland, this was now much reduced by the pact with Stalin and Hitler's hazy information on the political morale of the west. Poland was given an ultimatum which amounted to accepting German domination. Warsaw refused to comply with the demand to send a plenipotentiary to negotiate terms in Berlin. On the morning of 31 August German troops invaded Poland.

On the same day Mussolini, convinced by his advisers of Italian military weakness, made one last effort to avert a general war, in case Italy should be forced willy-nilly into the conflict. On 31 August he proposed a conference of the powers to resolve the outstanding issues of the Versailles Settlement, including Poland. France reacted enthusiastically and Britain showed interest, but both powers insisted that a condition for such a conference was the withdrawal of German troops from Polish soil. Count Ciano, the Italian foreign minister, could not bring himself to tell this to Hitler, and the idea of a conference collapsed [**doc. 24**]. Hitler saw in the west's delay confirmation that the Allies were trying to extricate themselves from the promise of help to Poland as he had expected, and ignored the British and French ultimata demanding an end to hostilities. After two days of final preparations for evacuation and mobilisation Britain declared war on Germany at 11 a.m. on 3 September, still hoping that Hitler might thus be deterred from taking further action [**doc. 25**]. Daladier had received a letter from Berlin on 31 August insisting that Hitler was on his knees and would back down if the west held firm (**33**). Buoyed up with this information, but with grave misgivings, he announced to the French Chamber of Deputies that France was at war from 5 p.m. on 3 September: 'In honouring our word we fight to defend our soil, our homes, our liberties' (**11a**).

Though neither power entered the war without a sense of uneasiness, there was none of the panic and uncertainty of August 1914, nor the enthusiasm. The prospect of war had been accepted months before, and repeatedly confirmed in the days leading up to the German invasion. Faced with a general war, Italy remained neutral, on the grounds that Germany would not provide her with the economic resources necessary for her to intervene effectively. There was consternation in Berlin that the west had called Hitler's bluff. Goering angrily telephoned Ribbentrop: 'Now you have your damned war.'

6 From European to World War

It is possible to argue that the war that broke out in 1939 was not simply a limited European war but a world war. The French and British empires rallied to support the home countries. Economic warfare was carried on against Germany across the world. The entry of Italy into the war in the summer of 1940 spread the physical area of conflict to Africa and the Middle East. Yet until 1941 the war was essentially about the domination of the European continent by the European great powers. Not until Germany attacked the Soviet Union in June 1941 and the Japanese attacked the United States in December of the same year did the war assume world proportions and become, as Hitler had always intended, a real contest for world power.

The war in the west

For the western powers the war against Hitler proved to be disastrous. The rapid defeat of Poland was not unexpected, as both the western powers had always recognised the military impossibility of doing anything in the short term to save Poland. For six months they conducted the war – the so-called 'Phoney War' – more or less along the lines they had hoped for. Both sides continued to undertake secret negotiations and soundings to see if agreement could be reached. Many Germans expected the Allies to abandon the war once Poland was beyond help, divided between Germany and Russia according to the terms of the Nazi-Soviet Pact. In October Hitler announced proposals for peace before the German Reichstag [doc. 26]. But neither side was willing to begin negotiations except on their own terms, a prospect that could not be entertained by either Germany or the Allies. Chamberlain clung to the hope that Germany would still be deterred by the sight of British and French military and economic strength. In October he told Roosevelt that Britain would not win 'by a complete and spectacular victory, but by convincing the Germans that they cannot win' (95, p. 165).

This was to be done, as the Allies had planned, by blockade and economic warfare, and by using their political influence to isolate Germany. Favourable agreements on war trade were reached with Spain, Greece, Holland, Belgium and Scandinavia. The British and French navies immediately began their efforts to place Germany in economic quarantine. Plans were laid to attack Germany at what were supposed to be her economic weak spots, the supply of iron ore from Sweden and the supply of oil from Romania and the Caucasus. The plans for oil show the general drift of Allied strategic thinking. In January 1940 the French Prime Minister instructed the armed forces to draw up plans for attacking Russian oil installations and interrupting Black Sea shipping which was supplying Hitler with vital raw materials. General Gamelin, French commander-in-chief, reported that the best method was to bomb the Caucasus oilfields and to stir up Muslim revolt against the Soviet government in southern Russia. In March Gamelin issued a statement to the effect that both oil and Swedish ore must be seized and cut off from Germany, with priority to be given to oil supplies, 'to make the economic stranglehold on Germany tighter'. But these were difficult schemes to put into practice, and preparations were interrupted when Germany invaded first Norway, thus protecting her iron ore supplies in Sweden, then France, which ended all thought by the Allies of immediate action in Russia (**139**).

In practice the blockade could not be operated effectively; and the Allies exaggerated the extent to which Germany's capacity or will for war would be affected in the short term by the loss of either Swedish iron ore or Russian oil. Allied military preparations were confused and poorly co-ordinated. Belgium refused to allow Allied troops to move to the Belgian-German border as had been hoped, so that the Maginot Line became at once more vulnerable than the French had planned because it could be outflanked to the north. Although there was plenty of intelligence available on German plans to attack and on German strength, the assault when it came was devastating in its speed and competence. Despite material superiority the Allies were defeated by the superior fighting skills and training of the German forces, the one factor that the Allies had failed to take sufficiently into account. As French defeat became imminent, Britain abandoned full military support in Europe and withdrew what forces she could to the final defence of southern England. On 22 June 1940 France signed an armistice, and German domination of Europe became fact.

For Britain this was the worst possible outcome. It exposed the extent of wishful thinking on the Allies' side about the strategy of blockade and containment. French and British power on the Continent was broken, and Britain, not Germany, faced the prospect of diplomatic isolation, even of blockade. The competence of the victory surprised even Hitler, who with his generals had been apprehensive about German chances in the campaign. As it turned out, German war preparations, though incomplete, had proved equal to a military contest with France. They reached their limit in the failure to defeat Britain from the air, or to launch invasion in the autumn of 1940. German forces and equipment had not been built up to face this task with much chance of success in 1940. But it nevertheless appeared that Britain was now weakened, perhaps fatally, as a great power. The German tone in the summer became more dictatorial. Britain was offered peace on humiliating terms. Plans were laid to reconstruct the colonial areas of Africa in Germany's favour. A New Order was declared in Europe. Germany began the task of co-ordinating the economic resources of the conquered areas into a single German-dominated economic bloc.

To make things worse Germany's Axis partners used the opportunity provided by German successes to advance their own imperial ambitions. Italy joined the war shortly before the defeat of France and launched an attack directed towards the Suez Canal and Britain's vital interests in the Middle East. In the Far East Japan used the opportunity of the defeat of Holland and France to put pressure on their colonial possessions in the Far East. In September 1940 Japanese troops were stationed in French Indo-China by agreement with the French authorities there. On 27 September 1940 the Axis powers signed a Tripartite Agreement to provide mutual assistance in the reconstruction of the international system [**doc. 27**].

In the latter part of 1940 Britain's position was undermined even further by the onset of economic crisis much along the lines predicted in 1939. The American ambassador in London reported that 'Britain is busted'. British officials urged on their American colleagues the need for greater American help, without which Britain would simply no longer be able to buy the raw materials, food and armaments needed to sustain the war. The American attitude to the conflict was from the outset to avoid any political or military involvement, while demonstrating in its economic policy sympathy for the Allied cause. Like Wilson before him,

Roosevelt dreamt of being able to bring peace in Europe by hosting a great congress of the powers. Until the German attack on France in May 1940 American leaders still thought that it might be possible to reach an agreement with Hitler if the Allies would modify their conditions for negotiations. Even after the defeat of France the United States refused to enter into any sort of undertaking which might be interpreted as a political commitment.

For Roosevelt there were the usual domestic political considerations. Though the Neutrality Act had been modified in November 1939 to allow the Allies to obtain more supplies, new restrictions were imposed in June 1940 in order to safeguard American rearmament, which was finally set in motion in May of that year. 1940 was election year in the United States and Roosevelt was well aware that he could not afford to alienate the isolationist sectors of the electorate by making too many concessions to the British position. When concessions were made they were on the basis of conditions very favourable to American interests, the eventuality that the British had feared in 1939. In August the British were given fifty destroyers in return for eight American naval and air bases on British colonial territory from Newfoundland to British Guiana. Increased credit for British purchases in America was granted only on the promise that Britain would liquidate all her remaining foreign assets as far as she could to pay for them, and would also transfer £42 million of gold reserves stored in South Africa. When the United States finally agreed to give Britain military equipment under a Lend-Lease agreement in February 1941, it was only on the understanding that Britain had finally exhausted all her ability to pay. Britain's continued capacity to prosecute the war now rested on American goodwill (**126**).

Barbarossa

In the summer of 1940 Hitler ordered the German armed forces to build up a huge army of 180 divisions, with 20 motorised and armoured divisions at its core, for the purpose of turning east against the Soviet Union. So successful had German forces proved to be that Hitler was now convinced that he could have his great war, originally scheduled for the mid-1940s, in 1940 and 1941 instead. Defeat of Russia first also fitted in with the time-scale and nature of German armaments policy. Though large new production plans were laid down for the air force and navy, they would not be ready to fight the Anglo-Saxon powers effectively for at least another two years. Army equipment on the other hand was already very great and was planned to reach even higher levels in 1941. Recent research has shown that far from contemplating the limited use of economic resources for war during this period, the Nazi leaders ordered the full transformation of the German economy for war [**doc. 28**]. The rate of increase of military spending in Germany was at its highest during 1940 and 1941 (**134**).

Hitler based his strategy on the assumption that Britain could safely be left in isolation to be defeated later once the Soviet Union had been destroyed. Defeat of Russia would free him from the fear of a major war on two fronts and would release Japan in the east to contain the United States and prevent American aid for Britain. Russia was also the promised land of German *Lebensraum*. Conquest of Russia opened up the real prospect of world dominion and would give Germany access to economic resources that the Anglo-Saxon powers could not match. After Russia it would be a short step to drive the British from the Middle East and the Mediterranean before turning to a final reckoning with the United States. Evidence supplied to Berlin suggested that Russia was militarily unprepared, enfeebled by Communist rule [**doc. 29**].

The armed forces were issued with instructions for the attack on Russia, code-named Operation Barbarossa, which was to be carried out in the summer of 1941. As it turned out, the plan's fantastic nature was compromised by the reality of events. British success in defeating Italian forces in North Africa compelled Hitler to intervene on Italy's behalf there. In the Balkans the pro-German Yugoslav government was overthrown, and Italy, which ·had launched an attack on Greece in October 1940, was facing defeat there as well. Germany was forced to move southwards before moving against the Soviet Union, holding up the operation until late June, which meant that German forces had much less time than had been expected before the onset of the Russian winter. The spread of German forces southwards meant a dispersion of military strength at a time when arms production in Germany was found to be much lower than planned, due to the inefficiency and muddle of the Nazi-dominated administration. The only factor weighing in the German favour was the failure of the Russian government to listen to all the warnings from its intelligence sources of an imminent German attack. Stalin could see no justification for it. Russian supplies were punctually sent to Germany. Hitler was bogged down in the west and south and could scarcely be expected to turn eastwards as late as the end of June. The element of surprise on the morning of 22 June was complete.

The German invasion of Russia ended the anxieties felt in London and Washington about the possibility of a German-Russian alliance to overthrow the existing world order. Russian policy in eastern Europe after September 1939 had lent weight to these fears. Stalin occupied eastern Poland as agreed in the Nazi-Soviet Pact. Between 25 September and 10 October 1939 the Baltic states were pressured into accepting Russian troops on their soil and became Soviet protectorates. In November 1939 Russia attacked Finland which had refused Soviet demands for military bases. These, too, were extracted by force. In June 1940, while Germany was involved in France, Stalin incorporated the Baltic states fully into the Soviet Union and forced Romania to cede Bessarabia and northern Bukovina, which had been taken from Russia in 1918. Stalin continued to put pressure on other eastern European states to come under Soviet influence, and, in the belief that his bargaining position with Hitler was strong, asked in November 1940 for Soviet influence at the Turkish Straits and the German recognition of Bulgaria as a virtual Soviet dependency [**doc. 30**]. The effect of these demands was to confirm Hitler in his determination to crush the Soviet Union, and aroused in the west all the mistrust and hostility towards Communism that had been temporarily suppressed in the summer of 1939 (**117**).

The war against Russia brought relief to Britain militarily as well. It was now possible for Britain to pursue a peripheral strategy in Africa and the Middle East, while building up large air defence forces at home and a bomber fleet to attack the German war economy. But the attack still left unresolved America's position in the conflict. The most the British could extract was a promise from Roosevelt in December 1940 that the United States would be 'the arsenal of democracy' and pledges in the Atlantic Charter signed in August 1941 on introducing self-determination and free trade in Europe if Britain should win. In the background American trade officials continued to work, as they had done since 1938, to undo Britain's commitment to imperial preference, a concession that Britain was finally compelled to make in February 1942. Roosevelt remained worried throughout 1941 about the effects of a military commitment on domestic opinion until it was certain that America's vital political interests were at stake. Morgenthau, the Treasury Secretary, argued for war in May. Roosevelt's reply was

'I am waiting to be pushed into this' (**95**, p. 204). The German-Russian war opened up new uncertainties. Some American leaders believed that Russia would be quickly defeated, a fact that America could do little to prevent, but which would profoundly alter the balance of power against her. Others, Roosevelt included, thought that Russia would resist Hitler and perhaps make American intervention in Europe unnecessary. British blockade and bombing could be expected to do the rest. Like Chamberlain before 1939, Roosevelt prepared for war while hoping that it could at all costs be avoided or fought for him by others (**56**).

The coming of world war

The United States was also deeply concerned about developments in the Far East. For many Americans the Pacific was a more important sphere of interest than Europe. They argued that the Japanese empire posed a greater immediate threat than did Nazi Germany. Since the outbreak of the European war, conditions in the Far East had continued to deteriorate for the western powers. Japan began a cautious move southwards against the poorly defended colonial empires. In September the French administration in Indo-China was forced to accept an effective Japanese protectorate. Thailand was compelled to offer Japan military bases and to become a virtual dependency. Japan now dominated the South China Sea, threatening Malaya, the Dutch East Indies and the Philippines, where there were American military bases. Some Japanese politicians opposed further expansion, for fear of driving the United States to war. But the military and their civilian political allies argued that Japan was still far from self-sufficient in vital raw materials and could not defend her empire successfully until these had been guaranteed. Further expansion was a necessary condition for retaining what had already been won. This argument became more pressing in July 1940 when the United States began a partial embargo on the export of iron and oil to Japan. Japanese leaders feared that an economic encirclement might be imposed on Japan before the new economic resources could be captured. During 1941 Japan's financial position deteriorated as well and by the summer she had nearly exhausted her foreign exchange reserves, which were necessary to fund the imports of strategic raw materials. At the same time arguments about foreign policy led the armed forces to impose authoritarian rule on Japan under the so-called 'New Structure' of government.

Domestic political conflict and economic crisis pushed Japan towards a policy of renewed expansion and a confrontation with the other Pacific powers (**48**).

The situation in Europe encouraged the Japanese military to seize an opportunity that might not present itself again. France was defeated and could do nothing to save her empire in the east. Britain, it was believed, was close to defeat, which would leave the United States with the possibility of a two-ocean war for which she was not militarily prepared. The only problem was the position of Russia. In April 1941 the Japanese signed a non-aggression pact in Moscow which brought temporary security to the north. The German attack on Russia in June made it even more unlikely that Russia would intervene to prevent Japan from moving southwards. There was also evidence that neither Britain nor the United States would be able or willing to resist further Japanese aggression. Once achieved, the southern empire would be a basis for negotiating with the west from a position of strength.

The British position in the Far East was militarily untenable. Britain, as a result, avoided doing anything that might incite the Japanese. The British even argued for giving Japan a free hand in China if that would divert her for the time being away from the British Empire. The United States, while objecting to such a blatant appeasement of Japan, nevertheless sought throughout 1940 and 1941 to find grounds for full negotiations with the Japanese on terms acceptable to both sides. It was hoped that the Japanese 'moderates' would be encouraged by signs of American willingness to talk into persuading the military to abandon expansion in favour of conciliation. This proved as empty a strategy as it had done with the German moderates, for not even the more conciliatory Japanese leaders were prepared at the time to consider forgoing any of the gains they had already made. Though unofficial American and Japanese negotiators drew up a Draft Agreement in April 1941 as a preliminary to formal talks, the Japanese would not undertake to end their aggression in China and the United States would not accept the 1938 New Order declaration as a starting point for discussion. Nevertheless America did not close the door on negotiation, a fact which the Japanese took as evidence that the United States was still very uncertain about risking war at all (**56**). There were strong similarities here with the crisis in Europe in the summer of 1939 when Hitler interpreted the British search for compromise as a sign of weakness.

United States strategy in the Far East was faced by a number of difficulties. Rearmament on any scale was initiated only in 1940. Priority was given to the defence of the American mainland. A slow trickle of forces and equipment moved out to American bases in the Far East. By December 1941 there were still only 35 modern bombers in the Philippines instead of the 100 promised. There were domestic political problems to contend with too. Conscription was approved in Congress by only 203 votes to 202, evidence of the still widespread support for isolationism and appeasement. There was pressure from within governing circles not to take any action which might be construed by the public as helping to preserve the British colonial empire, although Roosevelt and his military advisers were not in favour of a strategy which was directed only at Japan and which abandoned Britain. 'Our strategy of self-defence', wrote Roosevelt to the American ambassador in Tokyo, 'must be a global strategy' (**95**, p. 193). The military chiefs wanted a strategy if war came of 'Europe first', while a defensive line was held in the Pacific. But in public the impression had to be given that the government was not about to plunge into a European conflict while there existed a visible threat to American territory in the west. This dilemma led to a certain paralysis in American policy in the second half of 1941, which was detected by Japanese leaders as they assessed the right time to strike.

On 2 July 1941 the Japanese cabinet, dominated by the military, decided to complete the programme for the establishment of an Asian New Order, whatever the American reaction might be [**doc. 31**]. Indo-China was formally annexed. Military preparations for a possible war with the United States, which had begun in January, were now directed towards attacks on American positions in Hawaii and the Philippines, and on the major British base at Singapore. In October the new Prime Minister, General Tojo, put Japanese demands to the United States for a free hand in Asia. It was agreed in secret that, should America refuse, which was likely, war would be declared on 8 December. The oil situation for Japan was now critical. Admiral Yamamoto, commander of the Japanese navy, doubted that Japan could prosecute a war successfully unless it were declared as soon as possible. To make certain of capturing the 'southern region' and of holding a defensive perimeter around the new empire, the Japanese navy trained large numbers of specialist air crews based on Japan's aircraft-carriers, who would be used to inflict crippling damage on American and

British naval power. Japanese intelligence confirmed how poorly defended American and British positions were. German information suggested that Russia was on the point of defeat and Hitler hinted at help for the Japanese if they attacked the United States. The Japanese Emperor, Hirohito, was informed that Japan's future as a great power was at stake unless the favourable opportunity to strike were taken. 'If there were no war,' the chief of the naval staff Nagano told the emperor, 'the fate of the nation was sealed. Even if there is war, the country may be ruined. Nevertheless a nation which does not fight in this plight has lost its spirit and is already a doomed nation' (**57a**). On 29 November the final order was given for war. On 7 December Japanese aircraft attacked the American naval base at Pearl Harbour in Hawaii.

Four days later Hitler declared war on the United States. Roosevelt was thus released from the responsibility of taking his country into war against the wishes of large numbers of Americans, and ostensibly in the interest of the British Empire or Soviet Communism. German and Japanese action now threatened America's vital interests. There was no doubting in Washington that the war should be prosecuted with all the power at America's disposal.

Why did Hitler declare war on the United States when his other major enemies were still undefeated? There is much to be said for the case that Hitler had always intended at some stage to face the United States in a contest for world power, if Germany were successful in dominating Europe and defeating Russia. His attitude to America was coloured by the same self-deluding racialism that characterised all his foreign policy. America for Hitler was a decadent power, vitiated by poorer racial elements, blacks and Jews. Hitler and Goering were dismissive of American military power. American pacifism and isolationism were evidence of fundamental weaknesses (**117**). German military intelligence attempted to alert Hitler to the real economic strength of the United States, but its reports were deliberately suppressed. No doubt Hitler was also influenced by what he thought was the imminent defeat of Russia, which would release vast economic resources for use against the United States. Instructions went out to the arms industry to give priority after the defeat of Russia to an enormous increase in naval and aerial strength to be turned against the Anglo-Saxon powers. Though there was a wilful lack of realism in his reasoning, it is easy to see how Hitler, with his forces at the edge of Moscow and pushing towards Egypt, and with news of the destruction of the American Pacific fleet, must have felt that he held in his hand the prospect of German world power. There were, however, more mundane considerations. From a German point of view the United States had been close to belligerency for over a year. Economic warfare was already being conducted against Germany. Lend-Lease provided a stream of munitions and resources for Germany's enemies. In the Battle of the Atlantic America had been compelled through German attacks on American shipping to take a more active role. American troops and aircraft were stationed in Greenland and Iceland. Hitler could not see, as the British could, the strains in the Anglo-American relationship, and he interpreted the Atlantic Charter as a deliberate provocation in the face of German efforts to build the European New Order. By December 1941 there seemed a strong possibility that the United States would declare war formally on Germany. Ribbentrop told his state secretary at the Foreign Ministry that great powers did not wait to have war declared upon them.

The underlying irony was that the German declaration of war brought into the conflict the one state which in 1941 was capable of destroying the power that Germany already possessed. The entry into war of the United States filled that power vacuum in world affairs which the Axis powers had been tempted to occupy. When the war ended almost four years later America and the Soviet Union, not Germany, were the world's major powers.

Part Three: Assessment

7 Hitler's War?

Wars are the outcome of a lack of stability, real or perceived, in the conduct of relations between states. They have causes of a general kind which form the context in which decisions about a specific conflict are taken. These general causes are in this sense permissive factors, without which the conditions will not arise for a particular war. The cause of the Second World War was not just Hitler. The war was brought about by the interplay between specific factors, of which Hitler was one, and the more general causes making for instability in the international system.

These general causes can be traced back, as we have seen, to the strains placed on the diplomatic world in the late nineteenth century by the rise of nationalism, empire-building and industrial power. The First World War was fought to resolve these tensions but failed to do so. The major victors, Britain and France, rearranged Europe at the end of the war in an effort to re-establish equilibrium in world affairs. Having done so they became committed, with some minor qualifications, to the *status quo*. Weakened by the war, and declining relatively in economic strength, both powers were faced by a galaxy of states and political forces opposed, for one reason or another, to the *status quo*. These included not only the defeated powers, but also Japan in the Far East, Italy in the Mediterranean and, of greater significance, both Russia and the United States. Stalin explained this to the British Ambassador in 1940: 'The USSR had wanted to change the old equilibrium ... but England and France had wanted to preserve it' (**117**, p. 7). In America the post-war settlement was regarded as a victory for old-fashioned imperialism. Though they expressed their opinions less bluntly than Stalin, American statesmen shared the same loose assumption about altering the equilibrium by undermining colonialism and reorganising the world economic system.

In assessing the causes of the war we might well ask why Russia and the United States did not impose their own idea of equilibrium at a stage earlier than 1945. The answer lay partly in the fact that until the world depression it was not entirely clear that Britain and

France, in co-operation with other League powers, could not make the Versailles system work. But it lay principally in the fact that for compelling reasons in domestic politics neither Russia nor the United States was in a position to exert its influence with any profound effect in world affairs. American isolationism and, after 1935, declared neutrality, and the need to consolidate Communist power inside Russia, held both states back from major intervention in international politics. Nor, it should be added, was Europe prepared to abandon its traditional position at the centre of the world stage. Europe possessed a wealth of diplomatic experience, commercial strength and political influence. Its moral ascendancy was taken for granted.

In practice European influence, and in particular that of Britain and France, was in decline. After 1932 the post-war settlement began to break down. Incoherently and uncertainly at first, a reordering was set in motion. It was spurred on by economic crisis and the deep resentments and hostility engendered by 'beggar my neighbour' policies. Great importance must be attached to the changing 'mentality' of international conduct in the 1930s. Fixed points in the system gradually gave way, giving the widespread appearance of dissolution and collapse and reviving fears of general war. From 1935 onwards war of some kind, civil war or invasion, was being fought in one or other part of the world. As the international system relapsed into increasing chaos there inevitably emerged at certain points specific ambitions to take advantage of the crisis. In Germany, Japan and Italy were political forces strongly influenced by social-Darwinist, nationalist ideology, which stood to gain by any change in the international distribution of power. All these movements expressed a clear commitment to expansion and war to achieve what they wanted. But all three states remained trapped in the framework imposed by the major imperial powers. It was assumed in each country, and not simply by its leaders, that colonies, empire-building, the scramble for possession of economic spoils, were perennial features of the world system. Domestic nationalism was translated into conventional demands for empire and spheres of influence.

As the weaknesses of the system were exposed, those states with plans for readjustment were tempted to go further. The isolation of America and Russia, with their tacit acceptance of changes in the *status quo*, provided further encouragement. Britain and France were both forced to decide whether or not to contest this challenge, and under what circumstances. Very little could be done without rearmament, but there was a certain flexibility in the system which allowed concessions to be made to all three aggressor states within terms acceptable to British and French interests. Active confrontation was postponed for as long as possible to allow their military strength to build up and to avoid domestic crisis at home, and also because it was not then apparent, as it is now to historians, what the ambitions of the three powers were. For much of the time Soviet Russia was distrusted as much as Germany. Neither Britain nor France wished to weaken Europe to the extent that Russia might benefit. Only when it became clear that Germany posed a real threat to British and French interests and could no longer be accommodated without destroying their status as great powers did they decide that war was necessary. Economic and military preparations, which provoked growing domestic crisis, pointed to the desirability of confronting Germany in 1939 by denying Hitler the free hand in eastern Europe which he thought he had won at Munich. Of course if Hitler had not decided to solve his 'Polish problem' in 1939, in the expectation that the Allies would now back down and accept the shift in the balance of power, the western powers would not have fought in September 1939. But they could now clearly see the implications for them of Hitler's appetite for expansion. At some point in 1939 or 1940 they were determined to confront him and enforce limits on German action, and had popular support at home to do so. Had everything gone according to plan and had Germany either backed down or been defeated by blockade and bombing, a not entirely unrealistic hope in 1939, Chamberlain might have achieved his grand settlement after all. It should not be forgotten that Britain and France went to war in 1939 in the expectation that this would be the outcome: that Germany could be defeated by the western powers on their own.

Could the war have been prevented? It is sometimes argued that it was feeble statesmanship that brought about war. Had Britain and France been prepared to confront the dictators sooner, even to the extent of fighting for the Rhineland in 1936 or the Sudetenland in 1938, then major war would never have been necessary. This is to ignore the reality confronting British and French leaders in the 1930s. They were faced with a confusion of different pressures both at home and abroad which at times must have appeared quite beyond the ability of even the most gifted statesman to resolve. As it was, they chose to find areas for compromise which did not fatally weaken British and French interests, as they saw them, while retaining political stability at home and the survival of their economic systems. It is wishful thinking to suppose, even if such things had been politically possible, that a display of strength in March 1936 by the western powers, or a higher level of arms spending in 1936 and 1937, would have very much reduced these pressures. It was not a lack of statesmanship that was at fault, but the basic weakness of the international structure which Britain and France were trying to salvage.

It has also been argued that the western powers misjudged the Polish crisis, that they should have allowed Hitler a free hand in eastern Europe, which would have brought him sooner or later into conflict with Russia, while throwing themselves on the mercy of the United States to restore stability in Europe and the Far East. This was, after all, what effectively happened between 1939 and 1941. But it ignores one crucial factor. Britain and France were determined to defend their status as great powers without resorting to dependence on either Russia or America. 'Pray God', wrote Cadogan, 'we shall never have to depend on the Soviet or the United States.' Theirs was an historic role, which could not be lightly abandoned. For so long the arbiters of world events, wealthy possessors of large empires, they both had a responsibility, a moral imperative, that required them to choose war rather than dishonour. If this seems a strangely archaic justification, it should be remembered, certainly in Britain's case, that most of the ruling class which dominated politics in the 1930s was infected with a sentimental and uncritical acceptance of Britain's role in the world derived from the heyday of Victorian imperial grandeur. This ruling class arrogated to itself the role of judging the national interest. Rather than face the reality of declining power, which had caused the crisis in the first place, it chose war.

Only the active and powerful intervention of Russia and the United States might have averted war in 1939. But instead, as the crisis deepened, Stalin began the years of purges and political upheaval which neutralised the Red Army in the eyes of Germany and Japan; and Roosevelt bowed to domestic pressure for neutrality. Both stood back in 1939, alive to the fact that some sort of revision of the international system was now inevitable, but both anxious to avoid war as long as possible. After 1939 the international system became increasingly fluid. Germany, Italy and Japan concerted their efforts to replace Anglo-French power after June 1940 by a solid structure of their own which neither Russia nor America could undermine. In the end, however, it became apparent first to Hitler, then to the Japanese military, that this new equilibrium could not be established without the military defeat of Russia and the United States, which meant world war. Once embarked upon their own imperialism, they were forced to accept what Britain and France had been reluctant to accept in 1939: that no defence or revision of the *status quo* was possible without involving Soviet and American interests, whether in eastern Europe, China or the Middle East. Hitler's invasion of Russia and Japan's attack on the United States were gambles for the highest stakes, the chance to achieve world power status at a critical point of transition in the international system.

It did not automatically follow that the final involvement of Russia and America in the war would bring to an end the brief two years of Axis ascendancy. But any realistic assessment of the strength of the two sides – and Britain's war effort was far from negligible – must conclude that it was only a question of time, and much bitter fighting, before a relative stability would be restored to the international system. This stability has been based since 1945 upon the balance of strength between the United States and the Soviet Union.

Part Four: Documents

document 1
The Covenant of the League

The High Contracting Parties,
In order to promote international co-operation and to achieve international peace and security

by the acceptance of obligations not to resort to war, by the prescription of open, just and honourable relations between nations,
by the firm establishment of the understandings of international law as the actual rule of conduct among Governments, and by the maintenance of justice and a scrupulous respect for all treaty obligations in the dealings of organized peoples with one another,

Agree to this Covenant of the League of Nations . . .

Article 8. The members of the League recognize that the maintenance of peace requires the reduction of national armaments to the lowest point consistent with national safety and the enforcement by common action of international obligations . . .
Article 10. The members of the League undertake to respect and preserve as against external aggression the territorial integrity and existing political independence of all members of the League . . .
Article 11. Any war or threat of war, whether immediately affecting any of the members of the League or not, is hereby declared a matter of concern to the whole League, and the League shall take any action that may be deemed wise and effectual to safeguard the peace of nations.

Treaty of Versailles, 28 June 1919, Part I, the Covenant of the League of Nations, in (8), pp. 59–60.

The search for a settlement

... the German visit was from my point of view a great success, because it achieved its object, that of creating an atmosphere in which it is possible to discuss with Germany the practical questions involved in a European settlement ... Both Hitler and Goering said separately, and emphatically, that they had no desire or intention of making war, and I think we may take this as correct, at any rate for the present. Of course they want to dominate Eastern Europe; they want as close a union with Austria as they can get without incorporating her in the Reich, and they want much the same things for the Sudetendeutsche as we did for the Uitlanders in the Transvaal.

They want Togoland and Kameruns. I am not quite sure where they stand about S.W. Africa; but they do not insist on Tanganyika, if they can be given some reasonably equivalent territory on the West Coast, possibly to be carved out of Belgian Congo and Angola. I think they would be prepared to come back to the League, if it were shorn of its compulsory powers, now clearly shown to be ineffective, and though Hitler was rather non-committal about disarmament, he did declare himself in favour of the abolition of bombing aeroplanes.

Now here, it seems to me, is a fair basis of discussion, though no doubt all these points bristle with difficulties. But I don't see why we shouldn't say to Germany, 'give us satisfactory assurances that you won't use force to deal with the Austrians and Czechoslovakians, and we will give you similar assurances that we won't use force to prevent the changes you want, if you can get them by peaceful means'.

Chamberlain memorandum, 26 November 1937, in (**58**), pp. 332–3.

American 'appeasement'

This country constantly and consistently advocates maintenance of peace. We advocate national and international self-restraint. We advocate abstinence by all nations from use of force in pursuit of policy and from interference in the internal affairs of other nations. We advocate adjustment of problems in international relations by processes of peaceful negotiation and agreement. We advocate faithful observance of international agreements. Upholding the principle of the sanctity of treaties, we believe in modification of provisions of treaties, when need therefore arises, by orderly processes carried out in a spirit of mutual helpfulness and accommodation.

Statement by Secretary of State Cordell Hull, 16 July 1937, in (**7**), vol 1, 1937, p. 700.

Stalin distrusts the west
document 4

One result of the protracted economic crisis has been the hitherto unprecedented tension in the political situation in capitalist countries, both within these countries and in their mutual relations. The intensified struggle for foreign markets, the disappearance of the last vestiges of free trade, prohibitive tariffs, trade war, currency war, dumping, and many other analagous measures which demonstrate extreme nationalism in economic policy have made the relations among the various countries extremely strained, have prepared the ground for military conflicts, and have put war on the order of the day as a means for a new redivision of the world and of spheres of influence in favour of the stronger States . . .

It is not surprising that bourgeois pacifism is now dragging out a miserable existence, and that idle talk of disarmament is giving way to 'business-like' talk about armament and rearmament. Again, as in 1914, the parties of bellicose imperialism, the parties of war and revenge, are coming into the foreground. Quite clearly things are heading for a new war . . . Still others, again, think that war should be organised against the USSR. Their plan is to defeat the USSR, divide up its territory, and profit at its expense. It would be a mistake to believe that it is only certain military circles in Japan who think this way. We know that similar plans are being hatched in the leading political circles of certain European states.

Report by Stalin to the 17th Congress of the CPSU, 26 January 1934, in (**2**), vol 3, pp. 65–8.

Agreement at Munich

It began by a brief statement by Herr Hitler thanking those present for their acceptances of his invitation and pointing out the need for speedy decisions. Mr Chamberlain replied suitably, as did M. Daladier and Signor Mussolini. Towards the close of his remarks Signor Mussolini said that he thought the best way of making progress was for someone to produce a basis for discussion, and he therefore read the Memorandum. It was evident that this document was a reasonable re-statement of much that had been discussed in the Anglo-French and the Anglo-German conversations, and the Prime Minister was ready to accept it as a basis of discussion by the Conference.

It was, however, the turn of M. Daladier to speak first, and to our relief he at once said he was prepared to adopt Signor Mussolini's document as a basis for discussion. This was agreed . . .

In the course of this discussion the Prime Minister raised the question of the representation at the Conference of the Czech Government. The conclusion was reached that the heads of the four Powers must accept responsibility for deciding – in the circumstances – how the situation should be dealt with . . . The German proposals for evacuation and occupation surprised us by their moderation and by the degree of latitude which they left to the International Commission. They were explained in detail by Herr Hitler by reference to a map, copies of which we were given.

After a short adjournment for dinner, agreement was reached upon the evacuation areas and upon the time-table.

We inserted in the preamble words to show that the Conference had been working in the light of the fact that it had already been agreed in principle that the Sudeten German areas should be ceded . . .

After very long delays due to inefficient organisation and lack of control, the Agreement and supplementaries were signed a little before 2 a.m. on the 30th September, and the proceedings concluded by brief expressions of satisfaction.

Note by Sir H. Wilson on the Munich Conference, 29–30 September 1938, in (**3**), 3rd Ser., vol 2, pp. 631–3.

document 6
Economic pressure on Japan

For about a hundred years up to the turn of the present century, when the principle of free trade was at its peak . . . if any nation adopted a protectionist policy in contradiction to the free trade policy of the Anglo-American powers, it was ostracized and considered a heretic by advanced countries. For many decades the less-advanced nations were not permitted to close their doors to the economic influences of Great Britain and the United States, and as a result, their industries were prevented from growing and attaining further development, being held back by advanced countries under political as well as economic pressure despite their will to progress.

When the doctrines of freedom of communications and trade prevailed the world over, enabling men and goods to move from one country to another with comparative ease, regardless of the status of their countries, it was possible even for small nations . . . to maintain a respectable existence side by side with great Powers . . . Now, however, that such doctrines have all but disappeared with the great Powers' closing or threatening to close their doors to others, small countries have no other choice left but to strive as best they can to form their own economic *blocs* or to found powerful states, lest their very existence be jeopardized. There can be no just criticism condemning this choice of the small countries . . .

Because of the existence of the idea of economic pressure, which does not seem likely to disappear, the countries which are not economically self-dependent will quite naturally try to find ways and means of defending themselves in anticipation of some crisis and in order to escape coercion in the form of economic pressure. They will consider the formation of economic *blocs* as a measure of economic self-defence, or the establishment of powerful states which can be self-sufficient both in times of peace and war . . . There is no reason why economic self-defence, which is the same [as military self-defence] in its ultimate effects, should not be acknowledged as proper in international relations.

Contemporary Japan, vol 10, January 1941, speech by ex-Foreign Minister Arita, reprinted in (**11**), pp. 74–5.

document 7
Mussolini's speech on victory in Ethiopia, 9 May 1936

Blackshirts of the Revolution, Italian men and women in the fatherland and in the world, listen!

Italy has her empire at last: a Fascist empire . . . because this is the goal towards which, during fourteen years, were spurred on the exuberant and disciplined energies of the young and dashing generations of Italy. An empire of peace, because Italy desires peace, for herself and for all men, and she decides upon war only when it is forced upon her by imperious, irrepressible necessities of life. An empire of civilization and humanity for all the populations of Abyssinia. That is the tradition of Rome, who, after victory, associated the peoples with her own destiny.

The Italian people has created the empire with its blood. It will fertilize it with its labour and will defend it against anybody whomsoever with its arms. In this supreme certainty raise up your weapons and your hearts, to salute after fifteen centuries the reappearance of the empire upon the fateful hills of Rome.

(**13**), 1935–36, pp. 471–2.

document 8
Hitler's dream of world power

'We need space', he almost shrieked, 'to make us independent of every possible political grouping and alliance. In the east, we must have mastery as far as the Caucasus and Iran. In the west, we need the French coast. We need Flanders and Holland. Above all we need Sweden. We must become a colonial power. We must have a sea power equal to that of Britain . . . We cannot, like Bismarck, limit ourselves to national aims. We must rule Europe or fall apart as a nation, fall back into the chaos of small states. Now do you understand why I cannot be limited, either in the east or in the west? . . .

'In the centre I shall place the steely core of a Greater Germany welded into an indissoluble unity. Then Austria, Bohemia and Moravia, western Poland. A block of one hundred million, indestructible, without a flaw, without an alien element, the firm foundation of our power. Then an eastern alliance: Poland, the Baltic States, the Ukraine, the Volga Basin, Georgia . . . We cannot in any way evade the final battle between German race ideals and pan-Slav mass ideals. Here yawns the eternal abyss which no mutual political interest can bridge. We must win the victory of German race-consciousness over the masses eternally fated to serve and obey. We alone can conquer the great continental space . . . We shall take this struggle upon us. It will open to us the door of permanent mastery of the world.'

Hitler in conversation with Hermann Rauschning, 1934, in (**32**), pp. 126–37.

Economic appeasement
document 9

But there are many who say that economic appeasement provides the key to our difficulties, and it is certain that with most of our political problems there is an economic problem inextricably intertwined . . . what is a serious danger is the extent to which Germany is moving away from the economic system of Western Europe into an idiosyncrasy of attitude not unlike that of Soviet Russia. To those countries who can supply her needs and will take her goods, such as the countries of the Danubian area, the Balkan States and Turkey, she acts as a strong attraction; and this is not without political danger. If this attraction were developed in the direction of Russia, who can supply so many German needs, the danger might become greater, and a division might establish itself between two economic systems in Western and Eastern Europe. It is, therefore, of urgent importance to restore Germany to her normal place in the Western European system.

Imperial Conference 1937, Memorandum by the Foreign Secretary, in (**89**), p. 164.

Britain and Germany in the Balkans
document 10

The Prime Minister
What, taking an economic view, is the position of Germany in relation to the States of Central and South-Eastern Europe? Geographically, she must occupy a dominating position there. She does now. As a matter of fact, in so far as those states are agricultural in character, the nature of the trade between them and Germany is complementary. They can supply Germany with raw

materials and foodstuffs in return for articles of manufacture which
Germany is so well fitted to supply, but I do not see any reason
why we should expect that a fundamental change is likely to take
place in those regions . . . So far as this country is concerned, we
have no wish to block Germany out from those countries or to
encircle her economically . . . Do not let us suppose that there
necessarily must be economic warfare between Germany and
ourselves . . . I finish what I have to say on this subject by the
general observation that, in my view, there is room both for
Germany and for us in trade with those countries and that neither
of us ought to try to obtain exclusive possession of their markets.

House of Commons Debate, 1 November 1938, in (1), pp. 338–9.

document 11
The Four-Year Plan

I hold it necessary that 100% self-sufficiency be introduced with
iron decisiveness in all the areas where this is possible, and through
this not only to make the national supply of these most important
materials independent of abroad, but that through this can be
saved that foreign exchange which we need in peacetime for
importing foodstuffs. I would like to emphasise that I see in this
task pure economic mobilisation, with no cutting back in armaments firms in peacetime for saving or stockpiling raw materials
for war . . . Almost four valuable years have gone by. There is no
doubt that we could be independent from abroad already today in
the areas of fuel, rubber and partly, too, in iron ore supply. Just
as we produce at the moment 7 or 800,000 tons of oil, so we can
produce 3 million tons. Just as we manufacture today a few thousand tons of rubber, we could produce 70 or 80,000 tons annually.
In the same way as we have increased from $2\frac{1}{2}$ million tons of iron
ore output to 7 million, we could process 20 or 25 million tons of
German iron ore, and if necessary 30. There has been enough time
to ascertain what we cannot do. It is now necessary to work out
what we can do.
 I therefore lay down the following task:
 I The German army must be ready for combat in 4 years
 II The German economy must be capable of war in 4 years.

Hitler's Memorandum on the tasks of the Four-Year Plan, August
1936, in Treue, W. (ed.) 'Denkschrift Hitlers über die Aufgaben

eines Vierjahresplans' *Vierteljahrshefte für Zeitgeschichte*, Institut für Zeitgeschichte, Munich, 1955, pp. 209–10, (translated by the author).

document 12
Economic dangers for Britain

We must face hard facts. We cannot finance ourselves by inflationary methods which, if they gave relief for a certain period to an embarrassed Exchequer, would be followed with certainty by a collapse in the purchasing power of our currency, so that the loans we could raise would represent little in buying power. We cannot continue to lose gold in great quantities indefinitely or we shall find ourselves in a position when we should be unable to wage any other war than a brief one. There is a limit to the rate at which we can raise money, and that limit to the best of my judgement, is already reached. We can go on for another six or nine months if there are no further additions, but thereafter, unless something unexpectedly favourable happens, it may well be that the present rate could not be maintained.

The Chancellor of the Exchequer, Sir John Simon, in Cabinet, 18 May 1939, in (**109**), pp. 276–7.

document 13
The crisis in France

The real trouble started on November 23 1938, first in the north of France, and on the afternoon of the 24th, in the Paris region. That day, while Mr. Chamberlain and Lord Halifax – who had already been welcomed at the Gare du Nord on the previous night with loud cries of *A bas Munich* and *Vive Eden!* – were being feted at the Paris Town Hall, a vast stay-in strike broke out at the Renault works with its 33,000 workers. Simultaneously, a number of other works were occupied. The stay-in strike at Renault's was a challenge to the Government; for no Government had ever even attempted to evacuate by armed force a factory even half that size. A year earlier M. Chautemps had sent the *garde mobile* to Colombes to evacuate the much smaller Goodrich Tyre works; but the strikers had threatened to resist; there was danger of serious bloodshed, and the Government withdrew the troops. The strike was ultimately settled after lengthy negotiations. But now there were no longer any Socialists in the Government; and M. Daladier, without even attempting to negotiate an evacuation, sent 10,000 *gardes mobiles* to the Renault works and ordered them to 'chuck the strikers out'. He told them, if necessary, to use tear gas. By midnight the works were cleared, with comparatively little bloodshed.

Werth, A. *France and Munich*, Hamish Hamilton, 1939, p. 370.

'Peace for our time' document 14

a) Anglo-German Declaration, 30 September 1938

We, the German Führer and Chancellor and the British Prime Minister, have had a further meeting today and are agreed in recognizing that the question of Anglo-German relations is of the first importance for the two countries and for Europe.

We regard the agreement signed last night, the Munich Agreement and the Anglo-German Naval Agreement as symbolic of the desire of our two peoples never to go to war with one another again.

We are resolved that the method of consultation shall be the method adopted to deal with any other questions that may concern our two countries, and we are determined to continue our efforts to remove possible sources of difference and thus to contribute to assure the peace of Europe.

(**1**), p. 189.

b) Franco-German Declaration, 6 December 1938

1. The German Government and the French Government fully share the conviction that peaceful and good neighbourly relations between Germany and France constitute one of the most essential elements in the consolidation of the situation in Europe and in the preservation of general peace. Both Governments will consequently do all within their power to assure the development in this direction of the relations between their countries.

(**6**), Ser. D, vol 4, p. 470.

The change of mood in the west

A year ago we had undertaken no specific commitments on the Continent of Europe beyond those which had then existed for some considerable time and are familiar to you all. Today we are bound by new agreements for mutual defence with Poland and Turkey: we have guaranteed assistance to Greece and Roumania against aggression, and we are now engaged with the Soviet Government in a negotiation, to which I hope there may very shortly be a successful issue, with a view to associating them with us for the defence of the States of Europe whose independence and neutrality may be threatened. We have assumed obligations, and are preparing to assume more, with full understanding of their consequences. We know that, if the security and independence of other countries are to disappear, our own security and our own independence will be gravely threatened. We know that, if international law and order is to be preserved, we must be prepared to fight in its defence.

In the past we have always stood out against the attempt by any single Power to dominate Europe at the expense of the liberties of other nations, and British policy is, therefore, only following the inevitable line of its own history, if such an attempt were to be made again . . . The threat of military force is holding the world to ransom, and our immediate task is to resist aggression. I would emphasise that tonight with all the strength at my command, so that nobody may misunderstand it.

Speech by Lord Halifax at Chatham House, 29 June 1939, in (**4**), pp. 58–65.

Hitler plans to crush Poland

Our situation *vis-à-vis* the surrounding world has remained the same. Germany was outside the circle of the Great Powers. A balance of power has been established without Germany's participation.

This balance is being disturbed by Germany claiming her vital rights and her reappearance in the circle of the Great Powers. All claims are regarded as 'breaking in' . . .

Living space proportionate to the greatness of the State is fundamental to every Power. One can do without it for a time but sooner or later the problems will have to be solved by hook or by crook. The alternatives are rise or decline. In fifteen or twenty years' time the solution will be forced upon us. No German statesman can shirk the problem for longer . . .

The Pole is not a fresh enemy. Poland will always be on the side of our adversaries. In spite of treaties of friendship Poland has always been bent on exploiting every opportunity against us.

It is not Danzig that is at stake. For us it is a matter of expanding our living space in the east and making food supplies secure and also solving the problem of the Baltic States. Food supplies can only be obtained from thinly populated areas. Over and above fertility, the thorough German cultivation will tremendously increase the produce.

No other openings can be seen in Europe . . . There is therefore no question of sparing Poland and we are left with the decision: *To attack Poland at the first suitable opportunity.*

We cannot expect a repetition of Czechoslovakia. There will be war. Our task is to isolate Poland. Success in isolating her will be decisive.

Therefore the Führer must reserve to himself the final order to strike. It must not come to a simultaneous showdown with the West (France and England).

Report on the Führer's conference with the heads of the armed forces, 23 May 1939, in (**6**), Ser. D, vol 6, pp. 575–6.

Chamberlain guarantees Poland
document 17

I am glad to take this opportunity of stating again the general policy of His Majesty's Government. They have constantly advocated the adjustment, by way of free negotiation between the parties concerned, of any differences that may arise between them. They consider that this is the natural and proper course where differences exist. In their opinion there should be no question incapable of solution by peaceful means and they would see no justification for the substitution of force or threats of force for the method of negotiation.

. . . I now have to inform the House that in the event of any action which clearly threatened Polish independence, and which the Polish government accordingly considered it vital to resist with their national forces, His Majesty's Government would feel themselves bound at once to lend the Polish Government all support in their power. They have given the Polish Government an assurance to this effect.

(**3**), 3rd Ser., vol 4, p. 553.

document 18
British intelligence on Germany

Let us examine firstly Germany's situation at the moment. From the point of view of the German Army it is extremely unsound. A considerable proportion of the active Army – unmobilised and in many cases under peace strength – is scattered throughout Moravia and Bohemia, with elements in Slovakia. It must be at least several months before the Germans can hope to produce units or formations with the help of arms they have acquired from the Czechs. The process will call for the services of many officers and NCOs who can ill be spared from the active German army ... If we can only convince our potential allies in the east of the patent fact that Germany is in no position to fight a major war now with any hope of evading inevitable and swift strangulation, there seems every reason why we should do our best to produce a situation leading to such a war and definitely welcome it. It is indeed, in my opinion, the only sound solution to the problem with which we are faced ... Nothing but the internal disruption of Germany can save us. Have we any right to consider such disruption more than an outside possibility?

It is true that grave elements of discontent within the country exist. But to produce the organised resistance to the Party or dissension within its ranks which can alone produce disruption, something more than a continuation or even an appreciable increase in the present perfectly bearable 'hardships' and inconveniences under which the German people suffer is required. War, and war now with a 'near' eastern front, would hit them hard and quickly and might well produce the hoped-for results. Without war, and with increasing benefits from Germany's eastern neighbours, these results may never be achieved.

Memorandum on the German military situation by the Military Attaché in Berlin, 28 March 1939, in (**3**), 3rd Ser., vol 4, pp. 623–7.

document 19

Stalin repudiates the West after Munich

Similarly, in matters of foreign policy, account is taken of the realities of the situation and, above all, of the fact that, in the present
state of the Red army, of the Soviet economic system and of Soviet
transport, the Soviet Union should avoid intervention in a conflict
of capitalistic powers. Thus, while M. Stalin and various other
speakers at the Congress emphasise Soviet readiness to defend the
frontiers of the Soviet Union, should they be attacked, the line
taken by all of them is that the chief care of those responsible for
Soviet foreign policy must be to prevent the Soviet Union from
being dragged into the struggle now in progress between the
Fascist states and the so-called democracies. M. Stalin did, of
course, say that the Soviet Union would be prepared to support
all peoples who had been the victims of aggression and who were
fighting for their national independence. This, however, may
merely imply that the Soviet Government would be prepared, as
in the case of China and Republican Spain, to provide assistance
in the form of war material, provisions and technical help, after
aggression was in full swing. Those innocents at home who believe
that Soviet Russia is only awaiting an invitation to join the
Western democracies should be advised to ponder M. Stalin's
advice to his party:-

'To be cautious and not allow Soviet Russia to be drawn into
conflicts by warmongers who are accustomed to have others pull
the chestnuts out of the fire.'

Report from the British Ambassador in Moscow to the Foreign
Secretary, 20 March 1939, in (**3**), 3rd Ser., vol 4, p. 419.

document 20

The Nazi-Soviet pact

23rd August 1939
Guided by the desire to strengthen the cause of peace between the
USSR and Germany, and proceeding from the fundamental stipu-
lations of the neutrality treaty concluded in April 1926, the
Government of the USSR and the Government of Germany have
come to the following agreement:

Article 1. The two contracting parties undertake to refrain from
any act of force, any aggressive act, or any attack against each

other, either individually or in conjunction with other Powers.

Article 2. If one of the contracting parties should become the object of hostilities on the part of a third Power, the other contracting party will give no support of any kind to that third Power.

Secret Additional Protocol

On the occasion of the signature of the non-aggression treaty between the German Reich and the USSR, the undersigned plenipotentiaries of the two parties discussed in strictly confidential conversations the question of the delimitation of their respective spheres of interest in Eastern Europe. These conversations led to the following result:

1. In the event of a territorial and political transformation in the territories belonging to the Baltic states, the northern frontier of Lithuania shall represent the frontier of the spheres of interest both of Germany and the USSR . . .

2. In the event of a territorial and political transformation of the territories belonging to the Polish State, the spheres of interest of both Germany and the USSR shall be bounded approximately by the line of the rivers Narev, Vistula and San . . .

3. With regard to South-Eastern Europe, the Soviet side emphasizes its interest in Bessarabia.

Treaty of Non-Aggression between the USSR and Germany, in (2), vol 3, pp. 359–61.

document 21
Hitler gambles on western weakness

Now it is also a great risk. Iron nerves, iron resolution.

The following special reasons strengthen my idea. England and France are obligated, neither is in a position for it. There is no actual rearmament in England, just propaganda . . . The English speak of a war of nerves. It is one element of this war of nerves to present an increase in armament. But how is British rearmament in actual fact? The construction programme of the Navy for 1938 has not yet been filled. Only mobilization of the reserve fleet. Purchase of fishing steamers. Considerable strengthening of the Navy, not before 1941 or 1942.

Little has been done on land. England will be able to send a maximum of 3 divisions to the continent. A little has been done for the air force, but it is only a beginning . . . England does not want the conflict to break out for two or three years . . . England's position in the world is very precarious. She will not accept any risks.

France lacks men (decline of the birth rate). Little has been done for rearmament. The artillery is antiquated. France did not want to enter on this adventure . . .

The enemy had another hope, that Russia would become our enemy after the conquest of Poland. The enemy did not count on my great power of resolution. Our enemies are little worms. I saw them at Munich.

Führer's speech to the commanders-in-chief, 22 August 1939, in (**10**), vol 3, pp. 584–5.

document 22
The last gasp of appeasement

21st July 1939
The programme discussed by Herr Wohlthat and Sir Horace Wilson was as follows: (a) political points; (b) military points; (c) economic points . . . Herr Wilson suggested as the general objective a broad Anglo-German agreement on all major questions, as had been originally envisaged by the Führer. In this way questions of such great importance would be raised and settled that the deadlocked Near Eastern questions, such as Danzig and Poland, would be pushed into the background and become immaterial. Sir Horace Wilson definitely told Herr Wohlthat that the conclusion of a non-aggression pact would enable Britain to rid herself of her commitments vis-à-vis Poland. As a result the Polish problem would lose much of its acuteness . . .

Sir Horace Wilson further said that it was contemplated holding new elections in Britain this autumn. From the point of view of purely domestic political tactics, it was all one to the Government whether the elections were held under the cry 'Be Ready for a Coming War!' or under the cry 'A Lasting Understanding With Germany in Prospect and Achievable!'. It could obtain the backing of the electors for either of these cries and assure its rule for another five years. Naturally, it preferred the peaceful cry.

Memorandum by the German Ambassador in London, von Dirksen, 21 July 1939, about unofficial conversations on an Anglo-German agreement, in (**13**), 1939–46, vol 1, pp. 324–6.

document 23
Poland in the middle

Following 'authoritative' indication was publication this morning of Polish attitude regarding Danzig. Poland would regard as a violation of her rights

    (a) any attempt to incorporate Danzig in Reich

    (b) exclusion of Danzig from Polish customs territory

    (c) control of Polish rights in Danzig by a third Power

    (d) deprivation of Polish minority in Danzig of rights of national development . . .

Attitude of Polish Government would depend on changes made. If their aim were contrary to any of these four fundamental points Polish Government would draw appropriate conclusions and act accordingly.

Sir H. Kennard in Warsaw to Lord Halifax, 25 August 1939, in (**3**), 3rd Ser., vol 7, pp. 236–7.

document 24
The last days of peace

August 31, 1939. An ugly awakening. Attolico* telegraphs at nine, saying that the situation is desperate and that unless something new comes up there will be war in a few hours. I go quickly to the Palazzo Venezia. We must find a new solution. In agreement with the Duce I telephone Halifax to tell him that the Duce can intervene with Hitler only if he brings a fat prize: Danzig. Empty handed he can do nothing . . . As a last resort let us propose to France and Great Britain a conference for September 5th, for the purpose of reviewing those clauses of the Treaty of Versailles which disturb Europe . . . Halifax receives it favourably, reserving the right to submit it to Chamberlain.

    Sept 2, 1939. Yielding to French pressure we suggest to Berlin the possibilities of a conference. A mere hint for the information of Berlin. Contrary to what I expected, Hitler does not reject the proposal absolutely. I inform the Duce. I call in the French and British ambassadors. I telephone personally to Lord Halifax and to Bonnet. I find much goodwill among the French, and maybe as much among the British, but with greater firmness. One

*Italian ambassador in Berlin

condition is put forward: the evacuation of the Polish territories occupied by the Germans.

It seems to me that nothing else need be done. It isn't my business to give Hitler advice that he would reject decisively, and maybe with contempt. . . . the last note of hope has died. Daladier talks to the French Chamber in a decisive tone, and his English colleagues do the same in London . . .

September 3, 1939. . . . At eleven o'clock the news arrives that Great Britain has declared war on Germany. France does the same at 5 p.m. . . . I am not a military man, I do not know how the war will develop, but I know one thing – it will develop, and it will be long, uncertain and relentless. The participation of Great Britain makes this certain. England has made this declaration to Hitler. The war can end only with Hitler's elimination or the defeat of Britain.

Excerpts from Count Ciano's diary, 31 August to 3 September 1939, in (**31**), pp. 140–4.

Chamberlain's 'awful Sunday' — document 25

September 10 1939

The final long-drawn-out agonies that preceded the actual declaration of war were as nearly unendurable as could be. We were anxious to bring things to a head, but there were three complications, – the secret communications that were going on with Goering and Hitler through a neutral intermediary, the conference proposal of Mussolini, and the French anxiety to postpone the actual declaration as long as possible, until they could evacuate their women and children, and mobilise their armies. There was very little of this that we could say in public . . .

The communications with Hitler and Goering looked rather promising at one time, but came to nothing in the end, as Hitler apparently got carried away by the prospect of a short war in Poland, and then a settlement . . . They gave the impression, probably with intention, that it was possible to persuade Hitler to accept a peaceful and reasonable solution of the Polish question, in order to get an Anglo-German agreement, which he continually declared to be his greatest ambition.

What happened to destroy this chance? Was Hitler merely talking through his hat, and deliberately deceiving us while he matured his schemes? I don't think so. There is good evidence that orders for the invasion on the 25th August were actually given and then cancelled at the last moment because H. wavered. With such an extraordinary creature one can only speculate. But I believe he did seriously contemplate an agreement with us, and that he worked seriously at proposals (subsequently broadcast) which to his one-track mind seemed almost fabulously generous. But at the last moment some brainstorm took possession of him – maybe Ribbentrop stirred it up – and once he had set his machine in motion, he couldn't stop it . . . Mussolini's proposals were, I think, a perfectly genuine attempt to stop war, not for any altruistic reasons, but because Italy was not in a state to go to war and exceedingly likely to get into trouble if other people did. But it was doomed to failure, because Hitler by that time was not prepared to hold his hand, unless he could get what he wanted without war. And we weren't prepared to give it to him . . .

So the war began, after a short and troubled night, and only the fact that one's mind works at three times its ordinary pace on such occasions enabled me to get through my broadcast, the formation of the war cabinet, the meeting of the House of Commons, and the preliminary orders on that awful Sunday, which the calendar tells me was this day a week ago . . .

Letter from the Prime Minister, in (**58**), pp. 416–17.

document 26

Berlin proposes peace

Berlin, October 6

Hitler delivered his much advertised 'peace proposals' in the Reichstag at noon to-day. I went over and watched the show. He delivered his 'peace proposals', and they were almost identical with those I've heard him offer from the same rostrum after every conquest he has made since the march into the Rhineland in 1936. . . . Hitler offered peace in the west if Britain and France stay out of Germany's *Lebensraum* in eastern Europe. The future of Poland he left in doubt, though he said Poland would never again endanger German interests. In other words, a slave Poland, similar to the present slave Bohemia.

Hitler was calmer than usual. There was much joviality but little enthusiasm among the rubber-stamp Reichstag deputies . . . Most of the deputies I talked to afterwards took for granted that peace was assured. It was a lovely fall day, cold and sunny, which seemed to contribute to everybody's good feelings.

William Shirer in his diary, 6 October 1939, in (**36**), pp. 185–6.

The Tripartite Pact
document 27

The Governments of Germany, Italy and Japan consider it the prerequisite of a lasting peace that every nation in the world shall receive the space to which it is entitled. They have, therefore, decided to stand by and co-operate with one another in their efforts in Greater East Asia and the regions of Europe respectively. In doing this it is their prime purpose to establish and maintain a new order of things . . .

Article 1. Japan recognizes and respects the leadership of Germany and Italy in the establishment of a new order in Europe.

Article 2. Germany and Italy recognize and respect the leadership of Japan in the establishment of a new order in Greater East Asia.

Article 3. Germany, Italy and Japan agree to co-operate in their efforts on aforesaid lines. They further undertake to assist one another with all political, economic, and military means, if one of the three Contracting Powers is attacked by a Power at present not involved in the European War or in the Chinese-Japanese conflict. . . .

Article 5. Germany, Italy, and Japan affirm that the above agreement affects in no way the political status existing at present between each of the three Contracting Parties and Soviet Russia.

Three-Power Pact between Germany, Italy, and Japan, signed at Berlin, 27 September 1940, in (**74**), p. 469.

Preparation for total mobilisation in Germany
document 28

The war requires the greatest efforts for building up armament. The High Command of the Armed Forces after consultation with the offices involved has recommended the following guidelines, which have as their object the strongest supply of economic resources in the service of national defence . . . Labour resources and factory capacity, which are not engaged with the production of war goods or essential goods, are to be made available insofar as they can be employed for strengthening armaments.

Goering decree 'on guidelines for the co-ordination of all resources to increase production for the armed forces', 29 November 1939, Speer Collection, Imperial War Museum, FD 5445/45.

document 29

The German attack on Russia

The Führer gives me a comprehensive explanation of the situation: the attack on Russia will begin as soon as all our troops are in position. This will be sometime in the course of next week. The campaign in Greece cost us dear in matériel, and this is why it is taking somewhat longer than anticipated. They have about 180–200 divisions at their disposal, perhaps rather fewer, in any case about the same as we. And so far as personnel and equipment are concerned, there is no comparison with our forces. The first thrust will be executed at various points. The enemy will be driven back in one, smooth movement. The Führer estimates that the operation will take four months, I reckon on fewer. Bolshevism will collapse like a house of cards. We face victories unequalled in human history.

We must act. Moscow intends to keep out of the war until Europe is exhausted and bled white. Then Stalin will move to bolshevise Europe and impose his own rule. We shall upset his calculations with one stroke . . . We shall fight until Russia's military power no longer exists. Japan is with us. The operation is also necessary from her point of view. Tokyo would never become involved with the USA with Russia intact to her rear. Another reason why Russia must be destroyed. England would like to maintain Russia as a surety for the future of Europe. That was the reason for Cripps' mission to Moscow. It failed. But Russia would attack us if we were weak, and then we would face a two-front war, which we are avoiding by this pre-emptive strike . . . The Führer says: right or wrong, we must win. It is the only way.

Goebbels in his diary, 16 June 1941, in (**37**), pp. 413–15.

document 30
Russia raises the price for co-operation

The Soviet Union is prepared to accept the draft of the Four-Power Pact which the Reich Foreign Minister outlined in the conversation of 13th November, regarding political collaboration and reciprocal economic support, subject to the following conditions:

1. Provided that the German troops are immediately withdrawn from Finland, which, under the agreements of 1939, belongs to the Soviet Union's sphere of influence . . .

2. Provided that within the next few months the security of the Soviet Union in the Straits is assured by the conclusion of a mutual assistance pact between the Soviet Union and Bulgaria, which geographically is situated inside the security zone of the Black Sea boundaries of the Soviet Union, and by the establishment of a base for land and naval forces of the USSR within range of the Bosphorus and the Dardanelles on a long-term lease.

3. Provided that the area south of Batum and Baku in the general direction of the Persian Gulf is recognized as the focal point of the aspirations of the Soviet Union.

Statement by Molotov to the German Ambassador on the proposed Four-Power Pact, 25 November 1940, in (**2**), vol 3, pp. 447–8.

document 31
Japan decides on war

Agenda 'Outline of National Policies in View of the Changing Situation'
Policy
1. Our Empire is determined to follow a policy that will result in the establishment of the Greater East Asia Co-prosperity Sphere and will thereby contribute to world peace, no matter what changes may occur in the world situation.
2. Our Empire will continue its efforts to effect a settlement of the China Incident, and will seek to establish a solid basis for the security and preservation of the nation. This will involve taking steps to advance south, and, depending on changes in the situation, will involve a settlement of the Northern Question as well.
3. Our Empire is determined to remove all obstacles in order to achieve the above mentioned objectives . . .

In order to achieve the above objectives, preparations for war with Great Britain and the United States will be made . . . In carrying out the plans outlined above, our Empire will not be deterred by the possibility of being involved in a war with Great Britain and the United States.

Imperial Conference, 2 July 1941, in (**9**), p. 78.

Bibliography

PRIMARY SOURCES
1   Chamberlain, N. *The Struggle for Peace*, Hutchinson, 1939.
2   Degras, J. (ed.) *Soviet Documents on Foreign Policy*, 3 vols, Oxford University Press, 1951–53.
3   *Documents on British Foreign Policy*, 2nd Ser. vols. 1–19, 3rd Ser. vols. 1–9, H.M.S.O., 1946–82.
4   *Documents concerning German-Polish Relations and the Outbreak of Hostilities between Britain and Germany*, H.M.S.O., 1939.
5   *Documents diplomatiques français*, Ser. 1, vols. 1–11, Ser. 2, vols. 1–15, Ministry of Foreign Affairs, Paris, 1963–81.
6   *Documents on German Foreign Policy*, Ser. C, vols. 1–6, Ser. D, vols. 1–13, H.M.S.O., 1949–83.
7   *Foreign Relations of the United States*, Department of State, Washington, 1933–41.
8   Grenville, J. (ed.) *The Major International Treaties 1914–1973*, Methuen, 1974.
9   Ike, N. (ed.) *Japan's Decision for War. Records of the 1941 Policy Conferences*, Stanford University Press, 1967.
10 International Military Tribunal, Nuremberg Trials, *Nazi Conspiracy and Aggression*, 8 vols, State Department, Washington D.C., 1947.
11 Lebra, J. C. *Japan's Greater East Asia Co-Prosperity Sphere in World War II: selected readings and documents*, Oxford University Press, 1975.
11a Ministère des Affaires Etrangères, *The French Yellow Book*, Hutchinson, 1940.
12 *The Public Papers and Addresses of Franklin D. Roosevelt*, 13 vols, Macmillan, 1938–50.
13 Royal Institute of International Affairs, *Documents on International Affairs*, Oxford University Press, 1929–54.

MEMOIRS, DIARIES AND CONTEMPORARY ACCOUNTS
14 Beck, J. *Dernier rapport; politique polonaise 1926–39*, Editions de la Baconnière, Neuchâtel, 1951.

15 Bonnet, G. *De Munich à la guerre; defense de la paix*, Plon, Paris, 1967.
16 Dahlerus, B. *The Last Attempt*, Hutchinson, 1948.
17 Dilks, D. (ed.) *The Diaries of Sir Alexander Cadogan*, Cassell, 1971.
18 Dirksen, H. von *Moscow, Tokyo, London: twenty years of German foreign policy*, Hutchinson, 1951.
19 Gladwyn, Lord *The Memoirs of Lord Gladwyn*, Weidenfeld and Nicolson, 1972.
20 Grew, J. C. *Ten Years in Japan*, Hammond, 1944.
21 Halifax, Lord. *Fulness of Days*, Collins, 1957.
22 Harvey, O. *The Diplomatic Diaries of Oliver Harvey 1937–1940*, ed. Harvey, J., Collins, 1970.
23 Henderson, N. *Failure of a Mission*, Hodder and Stoughton, 1940.
24 Hitler, A. *Hitler's Secret Book*, ed. Taylor, T., Grove Press, New York, 1961.
25 Hitler, A. *Mein Kampf*, ed. Watt, D.C., Hutchinson, 1969.
26 Hull, C. *Memoirs*, 2 vols, Hodder and Stoughton, 1948.
27 Leith-Ross, F. *Money Talks: Fifty Years of International Finance*, Hutchinson, 1968.
28 Lipski, J. *Diplomat in Berlin 1933–1939*, Columbia University Press, 1968.
29 Lukasiewicz, J. *Diplomat in Paris 1936–1939*, Columbia University Press, 1970.
30 Maisky, I. *Before the Storm: Recollections*, Hutchinson, 1944.
31 Muggeridge, M. (ed.) *Ciano's Diary 1938–1943*, Heinemann, 1947.
32 Rauschning, H. *Hitler Speaks*, Butterworth, 1939.
33 Reynaud, P. *In the Thick of the Fight 1930–1945*, Cassells, 1955.
34 Ribbentrop, J. von. *The Ribbentrop Memoirs*, Weidenfeld and Nicolson, 1954.
35 Schacht, H. *Account Settled*, Weidenfeld and Nicolson, 1949.
36 Shirer, W. *Berlin Diary 1934–1941*, Hamish Hamilton, 1941.
37 Taylor, F. (ed.) *The Goebbels Diaries 1939–1941*, Hamish Hamilton, 1982.
38 Templewood, Viscount. *Nine Troubled Years*, Collins, 1954.

SECONDARY SOURCES: BOOKS

39 Adamthwaite, A. *France and the Coming of the Second World War*, Frank Cass, 1977.

40 Adamthwaite, A. *The Making of the Second World War*, Allen and Unwin, 1977.

41 Andrew, C., Kanya-Forstner, A. *France Overseas. The Great War and the Climax of French Imperial Expansion*, Thames and Hudson, 1981.

42 Aster, S. *1939: the Making of the Second World War*, André Deutsch, 1973.

43 Barnett, C. *The Collapse of British Power*, Eyre Methuen, 1972.

44 Bethell, N. *The War Hitler Won*, Allen Lane, 1972.

45 Bialer, U. *The Shadow of the Bomber: the fear of air attack and British Politics 1932–1939*, Royal Historical Society, 1980.

46 Bond, B. *British Military Policy between the Wars*, Oxford University Press, 1980.

47 Bullock, A. *Hitler: a Study in Tyranny*, Penguin, 1962.

48 Butow, R. J. *Tojo and the Coming of the War*, Princeton University Press, 1961.

49 Carr, E. H. *International Relations between the Two World Wars*, Macmillan, 1947.

50 Carr, W. *Arms, Autarky and Aggression*, Edward Arnold, 1972.

51 Carroll, B. A. *Design for Total War: Arms and Economics in the Third Reich*, Mouton, The Hague, 1968.

52 Cienciala, A. *Poland and the Western Powers, 1938–9*, Routledge & Kegan Paul, 1968.

53 Crowley, J. B. *Japan's Quest for Autonomy: national security and foreign policy 1930–1938*, Princeton University Press, 1966.

54 Deist, W. *The Wehrmacht and German Rearmament*, Macmillan, 1981.

55 Dilks, D. (ed.) *Retreat from Power. Studies in Britain's Foreign Policy of the Twentieth Century*, 2 vols, Macmillan, 1981.

56 Divine, R. A. *The Reluctant Belligerent. American Entry into World War II*, John Wiley, New York, 1965.

57 Drummond, I. M. *Imperial Economic Policy 1917–1939*, George Allen and Unwin, 1974.

57a Dull, P. S., *A Battle History of the Imperial Japanese Navy 1941–1945*, Cambridge University Press, 1978.

58 Feiling, K. *The Life of Neville Chamberlain*, Macmillan, 1946.

59 Fox, J. P. *Germany and the Far Eastern Crisis 1931–1938*, Oxford University Press, 1982.

60 Frankenstein, R. *Le prix du réarmament français, 1935–1939*, Sorbonne, Paris, 1982.

61 Friedländer, S. *Prelude to Downfall: Hitler and the United States 1939–1941*, Chatto and Windus, 1967.

62 Gardner, L. C. *Economic Aspects of New Deal Diplomacy*, Beacon Press, Boston, 1971.

63 Gibbs, N. *Grand Strategy. Volume I: Rearmament Policy*, H.M.S.O., 1976.

64 Haggie, P. *Britannia at Bay: the defence of the British Empire against Japan 1931–1941*, Oxford University Press, 1981.

65 Haight, J. M. *American Aid to France 1938–1940*, Atheneum, New York, 1970.

66 Heinemann, J. L. *Hitler's First Foreign Minister*, Berkeley University Press, 1979.

67 Henig, R. B. *The League of Nations*, Oliver and Boyd, Edinburgh, 1973.

68 Herzstein, R. E. *When Nazi Dreams Come True*, Sphere Books, 1982.

69 Hildebrand, K. *The Foreign Policy of the Third Reich*, Batsford, 1973.

70 Hillgruber, A. *Germany and the Two World Wars*, Harvard University Press, 1981.

71 Hinsley, F. H. *Power and the Pursuit of Peace*, Cambridge University Press, 1969.

72 Homze, E. *Arming the Luftwaffe*, University of Nebraska Press, 1976.

73 Howard, M. *The Continental Commitment*, Temple Smith, 1972.

74 Jones, F. C. *Japan's New Order in East Asia*, Oxford University Press, 1954.

75 Kaiser, D. *Economic Diplomacy and the Origins of the Second World War*, Princeton University Press, 1980.

76 Kemp, T. *The French Economy 1913–1939*, Longman 1972.

77 Kindleberger, C. I. *The World in Depression 1929–1939*, Allen Lane, 1973.

78 Knox, M. *Mussolini Unleashed 1939–1941*, Cambridge University Press, 1983.

79 Langhorne, R. *The Collapse of the Concert of Europe. International Politics 1890–1914*, Macmillan, 1981.

80 Leach, B. *German Strategy against Russia 1939–1941*, Oxford University Press, 1973.

81 Lee, B. A. *Britain and the Sino-Japanese War 1937–39*, Stanford University Press, 1973.

82 Louis, W. R. *British Strategy in the Far East 1919–1939*, Oxford University Press, 1971.

83 Lowe, P. *Great Britain and the Origins of the Pacific War 1937–1941*, Oxford University Press, 1977.

84 Macdonald, C. *The United States, Britain and Appeasement 1936–1939*, Macmillan, 1981.

85 Mack Smith, D. *Mussolini's Roman Empire*, Longman, 1976.

86 Marks, S. *The Illusion of Peace: international relations in Europe 1918–1933*, Macmillan, 1979.

87 Middlemas, K. *Diplomacy of Illusion: the British Government and Germany 1937–1939*, Weidenfeld and Nicolson, 1972.

88 Milward, A. S. *The German Economy at War*, Athlone Press, 1965.

89 Mommsen, W., Kettenacker, L. (eds.) *The Fascist Challenge and the Policy of Appeasement*, George Allen and Unwin, 1983.

90 Néré, J. *The Foreign Policy of France from 1914–1945*, Routledge & Kegan Paul, 1975.

91 Newman, S. *March 1939: the British Guarantee to Poland*, Oxford University Press, 1976.

92 Nish, I. *Japanese Foreign Policy 1869–1942*, Routledge & Kegan Paul, 1977.

93 Northedge, F. S. *The Troubled Giant. Britain among the Great Powers 1916–1939*, London School of Economics, 1966.

94 Offner, A. A. *American Appeasement. United States Foreign Policy and Germany 1933–1938*, Harvard University Press, 1969.

95 Offner, A. A. *The Origins of the Second World War. American Foreign Policy and World Politics 1917–1941*, Praeger, New York, 1975.

96 Ovendale, R. *'Appeasement' and the English-Speaking World 1937–1939*, University of Wales Press, Cardiff, 1975.

97 Overy, R. J. *The Air War 1939–1945*, Europa, 1980.

98 Overy, R. J. *Goering: the 'Iron Man'*, Routledge & Kegan Paul, 1984.

99 Peden, G. C. *British Rearmament and the Treasury 1932–1939*, Scottish Academic Press, Edinburgh, 1979.

100 Porter, B. *The Lion's Share: a Short History of British Imperialism 1850–1970*, Longman, 1975.

101 Pratt, L. R. *East of Malta, West of Suez. Britain's Mediterranean Crisis 1936–1939*, Cambridge University Press, 1975.

102 Preston, A. *General Staffs and Diplomacy before the Second World War*, Croom Helm, 1978.

103 Reynolds, D. *The Creation of the Anglo-American Alliance 1937–1941*, Europa, 1981.

104 Robertson, E. *Hitler's Pre-War Policy and Military Plans*, Longman, 1963.

105 Robertson, E. *Mussolini as Empire-Builder*, Macmillan, 1977.

106 Robertson, E. (ed.) *The Origins of the Second World War*, Macmillan, 1971.

107 Rock, W., *British Appeasement in the 1930s*, Edward Arnold, 1977.

108 Schmidt, G. *England in der Krise: Grundzüge und Grundlagen der Britischen Appeasement-Politik*, Westdeutscher Verlag, Opladen, 1981.

109 Shay, R. *British Rearmament in the Thirties*, Princeton University Press, 1977.

110 Taylor, A. J. P. *The Origins of the Second World War*, Hamish Hamilton, 1961.

111 Teichova, A. *An Economic Background to Munich*, Cambridge University Press, 1974.

112 Thorne, C. *The Approach of War 1938–1939*, Macmillan, 1967.

113 Ulam, A. *Expansion and Coexistence: a History of Soviet Foreign Policy 1917–1967*, Secker and Warburg, 1968.

114 Watt, D. C. *Personalities and Politics*, Longman, 1965.

115 Weinberg, G. *The Foreign Policy of Hitler's Germany 1933–1936* University of Chicago Press, 1970.

116 Weinberg, G. *Hitler's Foreign Policy 1937–1939*, University of Chicago Press, 1980.

117 Weinberg, G. *World in the Balance*, New England University Press, 1981.

118 Wendt, B-J. *'Economic Appeasement': Handel und Finanz in der Britischen Deutschlandpolitik 1933–1939*, Bertelsmann Universitätsverlag, 1971.

119 Young, R. J. *In Command of France: French foreign policy and military planning 1933–1940*, Harvard University Press, 1978.

ARTICLES

120 Bullock, A. 'Hitler and the Origins of the Second World War', *Proceedings of the British Academy*, 53, 1967.

121 Coghlan, F. 'Armaments, Economic Policy and Appeasement: Background to British Foreign Policy 1931–7', *History*, 57, 1972.

122 Crozier, A. 'Imperial Decline and the Colonial Question in Anglo-German Relations 1919–1939', *European Studies Review*, 11, 1981.

123 Haslam, J. 'The Soviet Union and the Czech Crisis', *Journal of Contemporary History*, 14, 1979.

124 Hauner, M. 'Did Hitler want a World Dominion?', *Journal of Contemporary History*, 13, 1978.

125 Hillgruber, A. 'England's Place in Hitler's Plan for World Dominion', *Journal of Contemporary History*, 9, 1974.

126 Kimball, W. F. 'Beggar My Neighbour: American and British Interim Finance Crisis 1940–1941', *Journal of Economic History*, 29, 1969.

127 Macdonald, C. A. 'Economic Appeasement and the German "Moderates" 1937–1939', *Past & Present*, no. 56, 1972.

128 Manne, R. 'The British Decision for Alliance with Russia, May 1939', *Journal of Contemporary History*, 9, 1974.

129 Manne, R. 'Some British Light on the Nazi-Soviet Pact', *European Studies Review*, 11, 1981.

130 Mason, T. W. 'Some Origins of the Second World War', *Past & Present*, no. 29, 1964.

131 Michaelis, M. 'World Power Status or World Dominion?', *Historical Journal*, 15, 1972.

132 Offner, A. A. 'Appeasement Revisited. The US, Great Britain, and Germany 1933–1940', *Journal of American History*, 64, 1977.

133 Overy, R. J. 'The German pre-war aircraft production plans', *English Historical Review*, 90, 1975.

134 Overy, R. J. 'Hitler's War. and the German Economy: a Reinterpretation', *Economic History Review*, 2nd series, 35, 1982.

135 Parker, R. A. C. 'British Rearmament 1936–39: Treasury, trade unions and skilled labour', *English Historical Review*, 96, 1981.

136 Parker, R. A. C. 'The Pound Sterling, the American Treasury, and British Preparations for War 1938–39', *English Historical Review*, 98, 1983.

137 Peden, G. C. 'A Matter of Timing: the economic background to British foreign policy 1938–1939', *History*, 69, 1984.

138 Peden, G. C. 'Sir Warren Fisher and British Rearmament against Germany', *English Historical Review*, 94, 1979.

139 Richardson, C. O. 'French Plans for Allied Attacks on the Caucasus Oilfields, Jan-Apr. 1940', *French Historical Studies*, 8, 1973.

140 Schatz, A. W. 'The Anglo-American Trade Agreement and Cordell Hull's Search for Peace 1936–1938', *Journal of American History*, 57, 1970–71.

141 Simpson, A. E. 'The Struggle for Control of the German Economy 1936/37', *Journal of Modern History*, 21, 1959.

142 Tamchina, R. 'In Search of Common Causes. The Imperial

Conference of 1937', *Journal of Imperial and Commonwealth History*, 1, 1972.
143 Thomson, D. 'The Era of Violence', *New Cambridge Modern History*, vol. 12, Cambridge University Press, 1960.
144 Wark, W. 'British Intelligence on the German Air Force and Aircraft Industry 1933–1939', *Historical Journal*, 25, 1982.
145 Watt, D. C. 'The Initiation of the Negotiations leading to the Nazi-Soviet Pact: a Historical Problem' in Abramsky, C. (ed.) *Essays in Honour of E. H. Carr*, Macmillan, 1974.
146 Young, R. J. 'The Strategic Dream: French air doctrine in the inter-war period 1919–1939', *Journal of Contemporary History*, 9, 1974.
147 Young, R. J. 'La guerre de longue durée: some reflections on French strategy and diplomacy in the 1930s' in Preston, A. (ed.) *General Staffs and Diplomacy before the Second World .War*, Croom Helm, 1978.

A Guide to the Main People in the Text

BECK, Colonel Jozef, Polish Foreign Minister, 1932-Sept. 1939
BENES, Edouard, President of Czechoslovakia, 1935 to Oct. 1938
BONNET, Georges, French Foreign Minister, 1938 to Sept. 1939
CADOGAN, Sir Alexander, British Permanent Under-Secretary of State for Foreign Affairs, 1938–46
CHAMBERLAIN, Neville, British Chancellor of the Exchequer, 1931–7; Prime Minister 1937–40, and leader of the Conservative Party
CIANO, Count Galazzeo, Italian Foreign Minister, 1936–43
DALADIER, Edouard, French Prime Minister, April 1938 to March 1940; Foreign Minister, Sept. 1939-March 1940
EDEN, Anthony, British Foreign Secretary 1935 to Feb. 1938, when he resigned in protest at appeasement
GAMELIN, General Maurice, French Commander-in Chief and Chief of the General Staff, 1935–40
GOERING, Field Marshal Hermann, German Air Minister 1933–45; Commander-in-Chief of the Air German Force; Plenipotentiary for the Four Year Plan 1936–45
HALIFAX, Lord, British Foreign Secretary 1938–40
HANKEY, Sir Maurice, Secretary to the British Cabinet 1916–38; Minister without Portfolio, 1939–40
HITLER, Adolf, German Chancellor 1933–45; leader of the National Socialist (Nazi) Party; Supreme Head of the German Armed Forces 1938–45
HULL, Cordell, United States Secretary of State 1933–44
INSKIP, Sir Thomas, Minister for the Co-ordination of Defence 1937–9
LITVINOV, Maxim, Soviet Foreign Minister 1930–9
MOLOTOV, Vyacheslav, Soviet Foreign Minister, 1939–56
MUSSOLINI, Benito, Italian Prime Minister 1922–43; head of the Fascist Party; Foreign Minister 1932–6
RIBBENTROP, Joachim von, German Foreign Minister 1938–45; architect of the Nazi-Soviet Pact in 1939

ROOSEVELT, Franklin Delano, President of the United States, 1932–45

SCHACHT, Hjalmar, German Minister of Economics 1934–7; head of the Reichsbank, 1933–9

SIMON, Sir John, British Chancellor of the Exchequer 1937–40

STALIN, Josef, Secretary of the Communist Party of the Soviet Union, and effective head of state, 1924–53

TOJO, General Hideki, Japanese Prime Minister Oct. 1941 to July 1944

WILSON, Sir Horace, Chief Industrial Adviser to the British Government

Index

Index

RELATED TITLES

Anthony Wood, *The Russian Revolution*
Second Edition (1986)   0 582 35559 1

This study provides a concise history of the Revolution and analyses the relationship between the various social theories of the revolutionaries and the later course of events. It traces the heated arguments amongst left-wing groups from the years before the fall of the monarchy up to the propounding of the New Economic Policy by Lenin in 1921, and concludes by considering why the Bolsheviks succeeded in seizing and retaining power.

R. J. Overy, *The Inter-War Crisis 1919-1939*
(1994)   0 582 35379 3

This *Seminar Study* takes the reader through the tumultuous, uncertain years of the inter-war period. In it Richard Overy argues that the inter-war years were, at the time, perceived to be years of crisis across the world. The book seeks to explain why dictatorships came to supplant democracy - in Italy, Spain, Germany, the Baltic States, and the Balkans and why the world slid into war once more in 1939.

John Hiden, *The Weimar Republic*
Second Edition (1996)   0 582 28706 5

It is usually assumed that, thanks to the harsh terms of the Versailles Settlement, the Weimar Republic was doomed from the outset and that Hitler's rise to power was inevitable. In this succinct *Seminar Study* (now revised for the first time since 1974) Professor Hiden seeks to dispel this simplistic view. He examines the fundamental problems of the new state but also argues that it did make some progress in tackling the major political, social and economic problems facing it in the 1920s. The author concludes by showing how it was a complex interaction of many factors which finally brought Hitler to power.

D G Williamson, *The Third Reich*
Second Edition (1995)   0 582 20914 5

Revised and expanded, the Second Edition of this highly successful *Seminar Study* introduces readers to the historical phenomenon of

Hitler's Third Reich. The new edition includes two brand new chapters, one on Nazi policy towards the Jews between 1933 and 1939 and one on the Holocaust itself. Fully updated, the study remains as useful and as thought-provoking as ever.

Martin McCauley, *Stalin and Stalinism*
Second Edition (1995)   0 582 27658 6

Readers will welcome the Second Edition of one of the most popular books in the series. For the new edition the author re-examines the remarkable phenomenon of Stalin and "Stalinism" in the light of the latest research findings of the Russian archives. The book also takes into account the vigorous scholarly debate between the old, dominant totalitarian interpretation of Stalinism and the alternative school of thought put forward by the "social historians" in the 1980s.

Harry Browne, *Spain's Civil War*
Second Edition (1996)   0 582 28988 2

Harry Browne's accessible account of the Spanish Civil War has now been updated, and expanded, in the light of recent scholarship. In particular, there is now a fuller analysis of the politics of the Second Republic and the regional and social bases of Spain's political parties. There is also a more detailed account of the military conduct of the war, of the extent of international involvement, and of the means by which both sides, despite the Non-Intervention Agreement, were able to purchase arms abroad.

Martin McCauley, *The Origins of the Cold War 1941-1949*
Second Edition (1995)   0 582 27659 4

This popular study explores the key questions facing students. Who was responsible for the Cold War? Was it inevitable? Was Stalin genuinely interested in a post-war agreement? For the Second Edition Martin McCauley has revised and expanded his original text in the light of recent events - the ending of the Cold War, the collapse of Communism and the demise of the USSR in 1991.

Martin McCauley, *The Khrushchev Era, 1953-1964*
(1995)   0 582 27776 0

In this new study Martin McCauley explores all aspects of the Khrushchev era: including reforms in agriculture, economic policy, uprisings in Eastern Europe, the Cuban Missile Crisis of 1962, de-Stalinisation and Khrushchev's attempts to reform the Communist Party. The book will be greatly welcomed by history and politics alike.